An Inspector Calls

by J.B. Priestley

There's plenty of scandal in An Inspector Calls, but this CGP Text Guide has an impeccable reputation — it explains the characters, language, themes, historical background and more.

We've included bags of brilliant online extras too. There's a free Online Edition, tailored activities for all the big GCSE exam boards, and quizzes to test you on the whole play!

GCSE English
The Text Guide

Contents

Contents

You'll see **QR codes** on the Practice Question pages, which you can scan with any device. They'll take you to a set of **Sudden Fail Quizzes** for *An Inspector Calls*.

There are separate quizzes for the **Plot**, **Characters**, and **Context, Themes & Techniques** — or you can try the **full quiz**, which combines all of these topics. Just scan the QR code to give it a go!

P.S. You can also find these quizzes at **cgpbooks.co.uk/inspectorquiz**

Inspector Quiz

Published by CGP

Editors:
Claire Boulter, Holly Corfield-Carr, Emma Crighton, Robbie Driscoll, Luke von Kotze,
Anthony Muller, Rachael Powers and Adam Worster

Contributors:
Peter Needham and Kerry Kolbe

With thanks to Claire Boulter and John Sanders for the proofreading.
With thanks to Jan Greenway for the copyright research.

Acknowledgements:

Cover photograph & image on page 4 by Owen Howells with kind permission of The Torch Theatre, Milford Haven

*Photos of An Inspector Calls at Lamb's Players Theatre, Coronado, California / directed by Robert Smyth /
cast: Glynn Bedington, Jillian Frost, David Cochran Heath, Jon Lorenz, Colleen Kollar Smith, Lance Arthur Smith, Robert
Smyth / photos by Ken Jacques and Nathan Peirson*

*With thanks to Simon Gough Photography for permission to use the images on pages 3, 5, 6, 9, 10, 11, 12, 13, 22, 24,
25, 26, 28, 31, 41, 42, 43 & 48*

With thanks to Chesil Theatre Winchester for permission to use the images on pages 3 & 27

Images on pages 3, 4, 11, 12, 19, 20, 23, 26 & 49 used under license from Shutterstock.com

With thanks to Alamy for permission to use the images on pages 8, 21 & 24

With thanks to Mary Evans Picture Library for permission to use the images on pages 1, 2, 29 & 36

*Image on page 33: Women working in a factory (b/w photo) by English photographer, (20th century) National Army
Museum, London/The Bridgeman Art Library*

With thanks to iStock.com for permission to use the images on pages 3 & 32

With thanks to ArenaPAL for permission to use the images on pages 3 & 5

With thanks to TopFoto.co.uk for permission to use the image on page 50

With thanks to Getty Images for permission to use the image on page 39

ISBN: 978 1 84146 115 1

Printed by Elanders Ltd, Newcastle upon Tyne.

Clipart from Corel®

Introducing 'An Inspector Calls' and J.B. Priestley

An Inspector Calls is about society and class divides

- J.B. Priestley **wrote** *An Inspector Calls* in **1945**, during the Second World War, but he **set** the play in **1912**.

- In 1912, society wasn't **equal** — **people** with more **money** and from a **higher** class had more power.

- Priestley used the unequal society of **1912** as a setting to get people to think about **inequality** in **1945**.

An Inspector Calls has a strong message...

1) The audience knows that the characters' world is going to go through terrible changes. 1912 was just before the **First World War** — which began in 1914 and killed millions of people.

2) Priestley wrote *An Inspector Calls* to **challenge** his **audience** to think about how many more **disasters** lay ahead for them if they didn't learn from **past mistakes**.

A wounded soldier receives first aid in a trench during the Battle of the Somme, 1916.

The war years affected J.B. Priestley's life and writing

- *An Inspector Calls* was written near the end of the **Second World War**, so the audience would have seen how war **affected** everyone. Soldiers were returning from the war and **hoping** for a **better life**.

- *An Inspector Calls* asks the audience to **unite** to improve **society**.

1894	Born in **Bradford**.
1910	Left school and started work as a **clerk** at a wool firm.
1914-18	First World War. Priestley was **wounded** but survived.
1919-21	Studied for degree in modern history and politics at **Cambridge University**.
1922	Started work as a **journalist** in London.
1939	Second World War starts.
1940	Priestley presented a popular BBC **radio programme**, 'Postscripts', but his show was cancelled after members of the government decided Priestley's views were **too left-wing** (i.e. socialist).
1941-42	Priestley founded various **socialist organisations**.
1945	Second World War ends.
1984	Died, aged 89.

J. B. Priestley

For more about **socialism**, see p.36.

Background Information

The play's set in Brumley — a fictional town in the Midlands

Brumley is described as an **industrial** city in the **North Midlands**. In 1912, cities like this would have had **factories** and thousands of terraced houses for all the **factory workers**. Here are the **key locations** in the play:

Status and wealth kept the classes apart

© Mary Evans Picture Library

Women working in a carpet factory, 1902.

- In 1912 the **upper** and **middle classes** lived pretty **comfortably**. Many middle-class men were wealthy and powerful because they had **businesses** or **professional** jobs, e.g. doctors.

- The **working classes** had a very different life. They had to **work hard** for **little money**, often in **factories** owned by the middle classes.

- People were expected to **provide** for **themselves**, so **support** for those in need was **limited**.

- This made it **difficult** for working-class people to **help themselves** if they fell on **hard times**.

Who's Who in Brumley

Arthur Birling...

... is a successful businessman who is well respected in Brumley. He owns a factory and is head of the Birling family.

Sybil Birling...

... is Arthur's wife. She's obsessed with etiquette and her status in society.

Eric Birling...

... is the Birlings' son. He's a secret alcoholic who's going to inherit his father's business.

Gerald Croft...

... is an upper-class businessman. He's about thirty, and is engaged to Sheila.

Sheila Birling...

... is the Birlings' daughter. She's in her early twenties, and is engaged to Gerald.

Edna...

... is the Birlings' parlour maid. She doesn't have many lines, but she welcomes the Inspector into the house. She's the only working-class woman on stage.

The Inspector...

... is a mysterious man who claims to be a police inspector. He's investigating the death of Eva Smith.

Eva Smith/Daisy Renton...

... is the victim of the play. We never see her. She might be lots of different girls. She might not even be dead...

Introduction

'An Inspector Calls' — Plot Summary

'An Inspector Calls'... what happens when?

Here's a little recap of the **main events** of An Inspector Calls. It's a good idea to learn **what happens when**, so that you know exactly how the plot progresses and how all the important events fit together.

Act One — one spring evening in 1912...

Photo: An Inspector Calls, ©2010 Lamb's Players Theatre

- The **Birling family** are celebrating Sheila's **engagement** to Gerald. It all seems to be going well, but Sheila **suspects** that Gerald lost interest in her last summer.

- Arthur gives a speech to Eric and Gerald about **business**. He says that every man should **look after himself**.

- Inspector Goole arrives and says that a **woman** called **Eva Smith** has **taken her own life** by drinking disinfectant. He starts to question the family members, one by one.

- It turns out Arthur Birling **sacked** Eva Smith from his factory for **striking** in **protest** against **low wages** and that Sheila asked for Eva Smith to be **sacked** from a department store last year.

- The Inspector explains that **Eva Smith** then **changed** her name to **Daisy Renton**. Gerald appears shocked and Eric leaves.

Act Two — everyone's tangled up in the Inspector's investigation

- Although he wants to keep it a secret, Gerald eventually describes how he spent last summer with Daisy Renton — she was his **mistress**.

- Gerald is upset. Sheila **returns** his ring and Gerald leaves.

- The Inspector gets Sybil to confess that she **persuaded** the **Women's Charity Organisation** to **reject** Eva/Daisy's appeal for help. Eva/Daisy was **pregnant** at the time.

- Sybil **blames** the **father** of Eva/Daisy's child for her death.

- Sheila guesses that the father of the child is **Eric**.

© Alastair Muir/Shutterstock

Act Three — Eric brings shame to the family

- Eric returns. He knows that the Inspector has led everyone to the **conclusion** that he's the **father** of Eva/Daisy's **unborn child**.

- He describes how he met Eva Smith at a bar, and drunkenly **forced** her to have **sex**. He got her pregnant and then **stole money** from his father's office to **support** her.

- Eva/Daisy **rejected** the **stolen money** and turned to Sybil's charity for help. Eric says Sybil **murdered** her own grandchild by refusing to give her **charity**.

- The Inspector reminds the Birlings that we are all **responsible** for each other. He warns that unless everyone **learns** to look after each other, the **lesson** will have to be learnt later with **greater suffering**.

Act Three — the final twist...

- Gerald returns, having spoken to a police officer who **doesn't recognise** the name 'Goole'. Birling calls the police station to confirm there is **no inspector** called 'Goole' in the area.

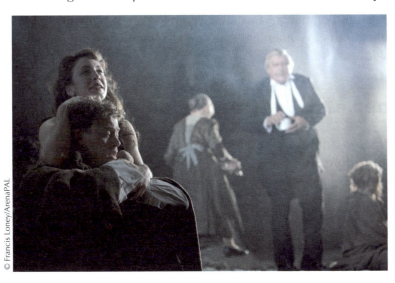

- Gerald calls the hospital and finds out that no one has **died by suicide**. Birling, Sybil and Gerald decide it's all been a **hoax** and start to **relax**.

- Sheila and Eric argue that they are all still **guilty** of treating someone badly.

- The phone **rings**. A young woman has just been found **dead** after drinking disinfectant, and the police are sending an inspector to **question** the Birling family...

Ring, ring — this is your future self calling...

...to say thanks for starting off your revision so well. Once you're confident you know **what happens when** in *An Inspector Calls*, turn over the page to start **Section One** for some cracking **analysis** of the **plot**. If you're still not 100% clear on the plot, turn to the back of the book for the cartoon...

Analysis of Act One — Arthur's Speech

After getting to know Priestley and pinning down the plot, it's about time to work out what's really going on. This section will analyse the play, act by act, pointing out key plot points and explaining the play's themes.

The Birlings are having an engagement party

1) Everyone is **content** and saying the **right things**.

2) The Birlings are Priestley's **idea** of a 'perfect' **middle-class** family:

© Simon Gough Photography

- the father's a successful **businessman**

- the mother works hard to keep up the Birlings' **reputation** in the community

- the son **works** for the father in the **family business**

- the daughter's **engaged** to the son of their **competitor** — this should **improve the business** because the two companies could start "**working together**" in the future

But there are hints of conflict under the surface

1) Gerald's family, the Crofts, are **more established** and **socially superior**. This makes Arthur Birling anxious.

2) Gerald says he was **busy** with work last summer. But Sheila's **not really satisfied** with this answer — "**Yes, that's what _you_ say** ".

3) There are **big differences** between what's expected of **men** and **women**. In this society, men are supposed to be busy with **work** and the world of **public affairs**. Women are supposed to be interested in **family**, **clothes** and **social etiquette** ('proper' behaviour).

Birling lectures the young men about war and business

KEY EVENT

1) Arthur Birling's **confident** about the future for his family and business. He gives a **speech** with his **predictions** for the **future**. But the audience of **1946** knows what's coming, and it's not what Birling thinks:

- He says **conflicts** between workers and bosses will come to **nothing**. But there were many strikes between 1912 and 1945, including the **General Strike** of 1926, which saw the country grind to a halt for nine days.

- He says technological progress will continue, and gives the recently completed Titanic as an example. He says it's "**unsinkable, absolutely unsinkable**".

- Eric asks whether there'll be a **war** with Germany. Arthur says **no way**. But two years later, along comes **World War One** — war with Germany.

2) Priestley uses dramatic irony to make Birling look **overconfident**. It makes the audience think that Birling might be wrong about lots of other things, such as his belief in the motto '**Every man for himself**'.

Writer's Technique

When the audience **know more** about something than the character on stage, it's called **dramatic irony** (see page 50).

Analysis of Act One — The Inspector Begins

An inspector calls and says a girl has died

1) The Inspector gives a blunt account of Eva Smith's death.

2) The harsh language — "Burnt her inside out" — contrasts violently with the polite and playful atmosphere at the start. The Inspector catches the Birlings off-guard, which helps his investigation.

3) The Inspector shows a photograph to Birling but doesn't show it to either Gerald or Eric. This is important because Gerald later suspects that each person was shown a different photograph, believing it to be the same one.

Theme — Family Life

The Birlings' family life is held together by secrets and polite behaviour. The Inspector disrupts everything and lets the secrets out.

Birling sacked Eva Smith to protect his business

1) The Inspector gets Birling to tell the story of why he sacked Eva Smith. This gives Birling a false sense of being in charge for a bit.

2) The workers at the Birling factory went on strike after Birling refused a pay rise. He wanted to protect his profits and prevent another strike, so he sacked the "ring-leaders", including Eva Smith.

3) This story gives the play a political element. Priestley's positioning the rights of the workers against the interests of the businessman.

4) Eva's described as a "lively good-looking girl". She's remembered as an attractive hero — this makes Birling look worse.

Theme — Social Responsibility

Birling sees employees as "cheap labour". If he can get them to work for less, he will do. He wants the opposite of 'social responsibility' — maximum profit for the individual.

Then Sheila got her sacked from her next job

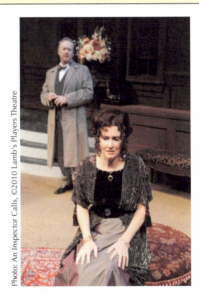

Photo: An Inspector Calls, ©2010 Lamb's Players Theatre

1) Sheila's shown a photograph — possibly not the same one that Birling saw. She recognises the woman she got sacked from Milwards last year.

2) Sheila's insecurity and jealousy made her think that Eva Smith was laughing at her at Milwards.

3) As a regular customer from a good family she had the power to demand that Eva Smith be sacked from her job. Sheila abused her influence.

4) But Sheila also says she "felt rotten about it at the time", and her reaction to the Inspector's news shows that she knew she behaved badly and that she's grown up a bit since then. Priestley portrays Sheila as a forgivable character.

Talk about the change of mood once the Inspector arrives...

It'll impress the examiner if you mention that the play's mood dips after the doorbell rings. Priestley sets things up nicely for the arrival of the Inspector — things can't get any better, so they must get worse.

Analysis of Act One — Eva Smith is Daisy Renton

Priestley ends Act One with the Inspector's reappearance because it makes the audience wonder how much the Inspector already knows, and how much there is yet to find out. Priestley's keeping his audience alert.

Sheila and Eric are sympathetic

1) Eric points out the **hypocrisy** of sacking Eva Smith for asking for higher wages because the Birling company "<u>try for the highest possible prices</u>".

2) Eric and Sheila give **emotional responses** to the Inspector's story, while their parents show **no sympathy**.

3) Sheila's repeatedly told to leave the room by both her parents — she stays because she feels it's her **duty** to stay to hear the **whole story** and to find out who's **responsible**.

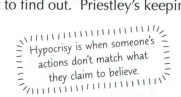
Hypocrisy is when someone's actions don't match what they claim to believe.

Theme — Young and Old

The Birlings don't think a young woman should hear this grim story. However, Sheila's a **young woman** who **thinks for herself** and **breaks away** from her parents' **traditional** views.

Eva Smith changes her name to Daisy Renton

1) The Inspector explains that after being sacked from Milwards Eva Smith decided to **change her name**.

   - Perhaps Eva Smith needed a **dramatic change** to **escape** her past.

   - Or maybe this is just the Inspector spinning a tale to **link** two separate women.

   - Either way, the name Daisy Renton's a **fresh** sounding name for a fresh start. But '**under the daisies**' was a **euphemism** for being **dead** (see p.50). And '**renting**' suggests **prostitution**. Maybe the name isn't so fresh after all.

2) Gerald is "<u>startled</u>" — he recognises the name.

© Everett Collection Inc /Alamy Stock Photo

Gerald confesses to Sheila

1) Eric and the Inspector leave to find Birling, giving Sheila the opportunity to **question Gerald**.

2) Gerald says his affair with Daisy was "<u>over and done with last summer</u>". He suggests that they should **keep it secret** so that it doesn't become a scandal.

3) Sheila's sure that the Inspector **knows everything** already — she's worried about "<u>how much he knows that we don't know yet</u>". Gerald and Sheila get more **anxious** and **suspicious**, which heightens the **tension**.

4) The Inspector **slowly opens** the door and looks "<u>searchingly</u>" as if he can read their expressions. He says only **one word** but it confirms that he's in **control** and **expects** something from them: "<u>Well?</u>"

Theme — Men and Women

It was **considered okay** for men to have affairs and mistresses. It wouldn't have been **acceptable** for Sheila to have a lover.

TARGET GRADE 8-9

After Gerald's confession, Sheila is described as looking at Gerald "*almost in triumph*" because she believes the Inspector is aware of Gerald's affair. This stage direction hints at Sheila's anger towards Gerald — it suggests she's pleased that Gerald will be judged by the Inspector, regardless of the potential consequences for their upcoming wedding and his reputation. You could also argue that it shows how, even early on in the play, Sheila has already chosen to side with the Inspector.

Analysis of Act Two — Gerald's Affair

The Inspector is piecing together the events of the final couple of years of Eva/Daisy's life. Act Two starts with the Inspector questioning Gerald about how he came to know Daisy.

Gerald kept Daisy as his mistress

1) Gerald **ignores** the Inspector's question, "**Well?**", and **excuses** Sheila for being "**hysterical**". He's trying to get Sheila to **leave** so he doesn't have to tell her more details about his **affair**.

2) The Inspector points out Gerald's **hypocrisy** in thinking that women should be "**protected**" when it's men like him who took advantage of Daisy Renton — "**one young woman who wasn't**" protected.

3) Gerald tells the others about his affair with Daisy. He defends the relationship — "**You know, it wasn't disgusting**", but Mrs Birling is **shocked**. She doesn't understand the term "**women of the town**" (prostitutes) and is upset to learn that Gerald's been seeing them.

Theme — Men and Women

If the Palace stalls are well known for being a place to pick up **prostitutes**, it's likely Gerald went there to find a prostitute himself.

Daisy fell in love with Gerald out of gratitude

1) Sheila suggests that Daisy loved Gerald as her "**wonderful Fairy Prince**". Gerald doesn't say he loved Daisy, but agrees that he "**adored**" being **loved** by her.

2) Gerald **finished** with Eva/Daisy just before he went on a business trip. Although he gave her some money, he effectively made her **homeless**.

3) Eva/Daisy went to a "**seaside place**" to remember their time together "**just to make it last longer**". For Gerald, it was a summer fling, but for Eva/Daisy "**there'd never be anything as good again**".

Gerald is shamed and Sheila breaks off the engagement

KEY EVENT

© Simon Gough Photography

Theme — Learning about Life

Although she's dazzled by the ring at first, Sheila's **mature** enough to realise the **consequences** of marrying a man who has **lied** to her.

1) Gerald should have confessed all this **months ago**. Less than an hour ago he said he hadn't seen Sheila much last summer because he was too busy at work. He **lied**.

2) Sheila says they'd "**have to start all over again, getting to know each other**".

3) Birling **defends** Gerald, saying, "**you must understand that a lot of young men —**". He implies that **lots of men** have mistresses.

4) Gerald doesn't ask Birling for permission to leave. He **asks** the Inspector. This shows that the Inspector's in **control** now, and not Birling.

 EXAM TIP

Mention the different characters' opinions of the affair...

Gerald's revelation doesn't shock Birling — he thinks it's OK for a man to have a mistress — but Sybil thinks it's "**disgusting**". Men and women in the play seem to have different opinions on what's acceptable.

Analysis of Act Two — Sybil Refused to Help

Priestley wants to show how lies underpin this family's life. Gerald's been lying about last summer, and Sybil's trying to avoid telling the truth. The fact that they're lying shows they know they've done wrong.

Sybil Birling is a hard nut to crack

1) The Inspector presents Sybil with the photograph. She pretends she doesn't **recognise** it.

2) Even when the Inspector manages to press the story out of her, Sybil won't accept any "**blame for it at all**" — she won't take responsibility for her actions.

3) Sybil can't **imagine** herself in a **similar situation** to Eva/Daisy — she can't **empathise**. Sybil is so obsessed with social class and reputation that she can't recognise **connections** between her life and anyone else's.

Theme — Young and Old

The Inspector increases the **tension** between the **parents** and **children** by using Sheila's help to get Sybil to tell the whole story.

Sybil had the last chance to help but she refused

KEY EVENT

1) Mrs Birling persuaded the committee to **turn down** Eva/Daisy's request because:

   - Eva/Daisy said her name was "Birling". Mrs Birling thought it was a "**piece of gross impertinence**" (rude) for Eva/Daisy to dare to associate her own scandal with the Birling family name.

   - She changed her story. At first she said her husband had **left her** and she was **pregnant**, but later admitted she **wasn't married**.

2) Priestley contrasts Sybil Birling's attempts to preserve her reputation with Eva/Daisy's moral standards. Eva/Daisy **wouldn't marry** the father of her child and wouldn't take any more money from him because:

   - He was a "**youngster — silly and wild and drinking too much**".

   - The money he'd been giving to her was **stolen**.

   - He didn't **love** her.

Theme — Social Class

Mrs Birling dismissed Eva/Daisy's story as "**ridiculous**" because she couldn't believe that a girl of "**that sort**" (working class) would ever refuse money. She based her refusal on **class prejudice**.

Sybil won't take responsibility

1) After trying to **resist** all the Inspector's questions, Mrs Birling realises that she can **blame** the father of the child instead of **admitting** her own guilt.

2) Sybil starts to tell everyone what she thinks should happen to **punish** this "**young man**".

3) Sybil blames the father for getting involved with a girl from a **different class**. She assumes she wouldn't know a man who **drinks** and **steals**.

4) She says that the Inspector should punish the man "**very severely**" before making him "**confess in public his responsibility**".

© Simon Gough Photography

Analysis of Act Two — Sybil Blames the Father

Mrs Birling really puts her foot in it

1) While Sybil is blaming the father of the child, the Inspector **doesn't intervene**, but instead lets her walk straight into a **trap** — demanding that he punish **her own son**.

2) This is the most **dramatic** result of questioning each person separately — Sybil answers the Inspector's questions, totally **unaware** of what Eric is going to say.

3) But Sheila is **open to the idea** that her family are **guilty** and guesses that Eric might well be the "**young man**" that Sybil's determined to **blame**.

© Simon Gough Photography

Sheila quickly sees what's going on

1) If the audience already think that Sheila has matured since the incident at Milwards, they realise that she's now a **very different Sheila** from the well-behaved and blushing bride-to-be of Act One.

2) Sheila can be **determined** and **stubborn** like her parents. But while her parents use their stubbornness to **resist** the Inspector, Sheila's **stubbornness** leads her to seek out the **truth**.

3) Sheila **demands** that Gerald and Sybil answer the Inspector's questions and tells Birling not to **interfere** when he's defending the behaviour of young men sleeping around.

> **Themes — Learning about Life**
>
> She recognised that she'd **changed** when she **handed** the ring back to Gerald, saying that they weren't "**the same people who sat down to dinner**".

Perfectly on cue — Eric walks in

KEY EVENT

> **Turning point in the action**
> All the major characters (except Gerald) are now on stage. Eric is forced to give a public confession.

© Alastair Muir/Shutterstock

1) Eric walks in, looking "*extremely pale and distressed*". It's as if he has been summoned to the dock, and his mother's already declared him guilty without knowing.

2) Eric's been **absent** for much of the play. He left the dining room in Act One and even left the house earlier in Act Two. Eric is always **running away** from his family and their **expectations** of him.

3) Act Two finishes with a **cliffhanger**. The audience is left wondering whether or not Eric was the "**drunken young idler**" who got Eva/Daisy **pregnant**.

KEY QUOTE **"No, he's giving us rope — so that we'll hang ourselves."**

Sheila's smart — she realises pretty quickly that the Birlings are all going to walk straight into the Inspector's trap. Mrs Birling dismisses her as over-excited, but she soon regrets not listening to what Sheila's saying...

Analysis of Act Three — Eric Confesses

The Inspector just had to open the cracks in the Birling family, and it's broken apart. Priestley carefully engineers the plot so that once the ball gets rolling, the family starts to self-destruct.

Eric confesses all — and it's a bit of a mess

1) Eric's **ready** to **confess**. He's guessed that the Inspector's helped everyone realise he's the father of Eva/Daisy's child — "**You know, don't you?**".

2) Eric explains that he forced Eva/Daisy to have sex with him, and got her pregnant — he was so **drunk** he threatened to cause a "**row**" if she didn't let him in to her flat.

3) He **regrets** his **actions**, but his **language** shows his immaturity. Eric calls Eva/Daisy "**a good sport**" and "**pretty**" — this sounds **insensitive** given how badly he treated her. Eric says that she treated him as a "**kid**".

4) Eric doesn't understand how middle-class men are **supposed** to behave. His parents think he's acted **worse** than Gerald, who knew how to have an **affair** without creating a **scandal** — but it makes the audience start **blaming** his **parents** for his upbringing.

> **TARGET GRADE 8-9**
>
> To his parents, Eric is a respectable young man, but in reality his actions are immoral and disreputable. You could link this to the separation between appearance and reality elsewhere in the play — for example, the Inspector appears real at first, but is later thought to be "a fraud", while Eva/Daisy appears to be one girl, but may be more than one.

Birling's appalled — not by suicide, but by theft and shame

© Simon Gough Photography

1) Arthur Birling starts to take the situation **seriously** for the first time. His son's **stolen money** from the company to help support Eva/Daisy, and Birling decides that he needs to "**cover this up**" as soon as he can.

2) In the middle of Eric's story, Arthur orders the **women** to **leave**.

3) Eric's involvement has gone **too far** for the Birling family. He'd have had an **illegitimate child** with a **prostitute**. This would have brought **shame** on the family.

Sybil returns and brings Eric bad news

1) Sybil and Sheila return to the dining room because Sybil "**had to know what's happening**" — she disobeys her husband now she realises how involved she is in the story.

2) Because Eric's been **outside**, he hasn't heard that Sybil was **involved** in Eva/Daisy's and his child's **death**. When he finds out he's furious, and links her failure to "**understand**" to his own **childhood** — "**You don't understand anything. You never did.**"

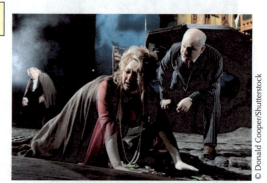

© Donald Cooper/Shutterstock

Some productions, such as Stephen Daldry's (as seen above), emphasise Sybil's reaction to discovering her role in her grandchild's death.

> **Themes — Family Life**
>
> Sybil's kept a polite household and a perfect **reputation** for the family, but at the **cost** of a **close** and **understanding** relationship with her children.

> **Turning point in the action**
> Every member of the family has let down their defences. They're primed and ready for the Inspector's speech...

Analysis of Act Three — The Inspector's Speech

The Inspector has his say

1) First, the Inspector **sums up** how **each person** at the dinner party **played their part** in Eva/Daisy's short life:

Arthur	**Sheila**	**Gerald**	**Eric**	**Sybil**
started it all by sacking Eva Smith	turned her out of her second job	kept her as his mistress and made her happy for a while	"used her" because he was drunk	refused her a "pitiable little bit of organized charity"

2) Now that the Inspector has broken through their **defences**, they're ready to hear his message.

- He **links** Eva/Daisy to the "**millions of Eva Smiths and John Smiths**" — the **rest of society**, or even the **rest of humanity**.

- He says everyone is "**intertwined**" and "**members of one body**" — everyone **shares** "**their hopes and fears, their suffering and chance of happiness**" because **everyone's affected**.

- He warns that if people don't **learn** to be more **responsible**, they'll be forced to understand their mistakes through "**fire and blood and anguish**". The Inspector's foreseeing all the **suffering** that will result from **selfishness**, including the **world wars**.

The Birling family structure collapses

1) The Inspector tells them at the start of Act Three that they'll have plenty of time to "**adjust**" their family **relationships**.

2) The first words after the Inspector's exit are Birling **blaming** Eric for their problems. This signals a **decline** from the Inspector's **moral speech** into **petty squabbling**.

3) Arthur Birling doesn't want anything to change. He's **desperate** to get things back to **how they were** — with him **in charge**.

© Simon Gough Photography

Everyone's ashamed — but not necessarily of themselves

Themes — Learning about Life

Birling says he's "**learnt plenty**", but not about how and why he's been wrong. He's learnt how Sheila and Eric **really behave** and **think**, and he's not impressed.

1) The word "**ashamed**" is passed between the family members. First **Sybil** tells Eric she's "**absolutely ashamed**" of his **drinking**.

2) **Eric** then says he's ashamed of his **parents' actions**.

3) Finally, **Sheila** says that she's ashamed of her **own actions**. She **shoulders the blame**, and asks everyone else to do the same.

4) The parents **haven't learnt anything**. They're more focused on trying to keep all the revelations **in the family**. The only thing they'd feel ashamed of is a **scandal**.

"We don't live alone. We are members of one body."

The play's coming to a close — it's usually time for the characters to learn their lessons. The Inspector does his best to make this happen, but not all of the Birlings are prepared to take responsibility for their actions.

Analysis of Act Three — Was it a Hoax?

Just when you think you've got it all worked out, there's a big twist. Apparently, Inspector Goole doesn't even exist — how do you explain that one? Then a final phone call tells us that there'll be no neat, happy ending...

The Inspector **might not** have been a **real inspector**

1) Sheila and Sybil realise the Inspector might be a **fake**, but they have different ideas about how important this is.

2) Sybil and Arthur agree that it makes "**all the difference**" if it wasn't a real police visit.

3) Sheila and Eric disagree — "**He was our police inspector all right**". It doesn't matter if the Inspector was **fake** if what he's shown them is true.

Photo: An Inspector Calls, ©2010 Lamb's Players Theatre

Gerald's return **splits** the family **further**

1) Gerald returns and says that he's found out there's **no Inspector Goole** on the force. Birling calls the police station to confirm that Goole wasn't a real inspector, and starts to think of the night's events as a **hoax**, with himself as the **victim**.

2) Sybil starts to **rewrite** her role in the evening — she says she's **proud** that she "**didn't give in to him**".

3) Gerald points out that the photograph might have been **different photographs** of **different girls**. Gerald calls the hospital and confirms that there's been no suicide — Birling is very relieved and considers himself **guilt-free**.

4) Gerald tells Sheila "**Everything's all right now**" while offering her the ring. She says it's "**too soon**" to be thinking about that and **forgetting** all she learnt this evening.

5) Gerald and Mr and Mrs Birling are relaxed and joking. The **atmosphere** seems just like it did at the start of the play — it's almost like a **happy ending**.

Writer's Technique

Priestley gives Gerald the **role** of a **detective** at the end of a **murder mystery** — he pieces together the events and **summarises** it for the others. But instead of **solving** the crime, Gerald makes it seem as if there was **no crime** at all.

A phone call... a **girl** has **died**, and an **inspector** will **call**

This news arrives with the same **spooky accuracy** as the Inspector's first arrival:

1) The Inspector first arrived **just after** Birling had said that "**a man has to mind his own business**". The Inspector's message was all about **social responsibility**.

2) And at the end of the play the phone rings **just after** Birling has **laughed** at "**the famous younger generation who know it all**". Birling still thinks *he* knows it all — he's **not learnt** the Inspector's lesson.

Mention the way different characters react...

There's a split in the way the characters react to the news that the Inspector isn't who he seemed. Mention that the elder Birlings and Gerald are relieved to get off scot-free — but Sheila and Eric still feel guilty.

Practice Questions

So, by now you should know *An Inspector Calls* pretty well, and be able to pick out important moments and details to help you analyse the plot. Try answering these quick questions in a line or two to make sure.

Quick Questions

Act One

1) How does the opening scene suggest that the Birlings are the 'perfect' family?

2) Before the Inspector arrives, Arthur Birling makes a speech about the state of the world. Name one event that the audience know will happen after 1912 which proves he's wrong.

3) Explain in your own words why Arthur Birling sacked Eva.

4) Why does Eric disagree with his father's decision to sack Eva?

5) Explain in your own words why Sheila Birling got Eva sacked.

6) Give two reasons why Priestley would have Eva Smith change her name to Daisy Renton.

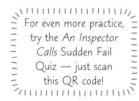 For even more practice, try the *An Inspector Calls* Sudden Fail Quiz — just scan this QR code!

 Inspector Quiz

Act Two

1) What word finishes Act One and begins Act Two?

2) How does Sheila react towards Gerald once he has finished telling his story?

3) Give one piece of evidence which suggests that Gerald's bad behaviour was quite common among middle-class men of the time.

4) Give two reasons why Sybil refused to help Eva/Daisy.

5) Who does Sybil say is ultimately the one responsible for Eva/Daisy's death?

6) Why does Sheila suspect that Eric might be the "young man" who got Eva/Daisy pregnant?

Act Three

1) Give two examples of language that Eric uses which suggests he's immature.

2) What piece of news makes Eric turn on his mother?

3) Summarise the Inspector's final speech in three main points.

4) Explain how each of the four family members react to his speech.

5) Why do the characters start to think that the Inspector might have been a fake?

6) Three telephone calls are made in Act Three. Say who makes each call, and what is revealed.

 What do you mean 'my nose is fake'?

Practice Questions

Feel like you're in the play — pretend that I'm the Inspector and I'm giving you a good grilling. Ah hello. May I come in? I've got a few questions for you. Yes, it concerns a certain play...

In-depth Questions

1) Think about your first impressions of Sheila in Act One.
   What sort of character did you expect her to be?

2) Do you think the Inspector planned to leave Sheila and Gerald alone together
   at the end of Act 1? How do you think this might benefit his investigation?

3) Mrs Birling persuaded her charity to refuse to help Eva/Daisy. In your own words,
   explain why she might have done this.

4) The Inspector questions Mrs Birling before he questions Eric. What do you think would
   have happened if Eric had still been in the room when Mrs Birling was explaining her
   role in Eva/Daisy's death?

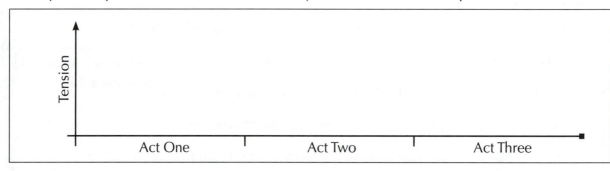

Has that Inspector gone yet?

5) Priestley puts 'cliffhangers' at the end of each act in the play.
   How do these sudden endings affect the audience?

6) Why do you think the Inspector leaves so abruptly after giving his final speech?

7) Why do you think Priestley adds the final twist, rather than ending
   the play with the discovery that there was no suicide victim?

8) Copy out the graph below. Draw a line that best represents the building of tension levels
   following these key events in the plot:

   a) Inspector's arrival   b) Gerald's confession   c) Eric's return
   d) Inspector's speech   e) Gerald's 'theory'   f) The final phone call

Tension

Act One   Act Two   Act Three

Practice Questions

You've read the play, you've answered the questions, you've got the t-shirt... Now all that's left to do is work your way through the questions below. Have a crack at the targeted 8-9 questions to really test your knowledge of the play and the exam-style questions to prepare you for what you'll come across in the actual exam.

Target Grade 8-9

1) In Act One, the Inspector says that it is "better to ask for the earth than to take it." What do you think he means by this? Explain your answer.

2) Do you think it's significant that Eva/Daisy has several different jobs and roles in society? Why do you think Priestley chooses to do this?

Exam-style Questions

1) Read Act One from Birling's line "**All right, Edna. Show him in here.**" to Eric's line "**My God!**". With reference to this passage and the play as a whole, discuss the mood in the Birling household and how it changes at various points in the play.

2) **Eric: The fact remains that I did what I did.**
   To what extent does Priestley present Eric as a forgivable character by the end of the play?

3) 'The Birlings, Gerald and the Inspector all describe Eva/Daisy in different ways.'
   How does Priestley use language to present the character of Eva/Daisy?

4) Write about the structure of *An Inspector Calls* and how it affects the mood and atmosphere of the play.

5) *Now Mrs Birling enters, briskly and self-confidently*
   What is the importance of characters' entrances and exits in *An Inspector Calls*?
   Think about:
   • when characters enter and exit the stage
   • how Priestley uses entrances and exits to create a particular mood.

6) How does Priestley change the way Sheila is presented over the course of the play?
   Think about:
   • how Priestley portrays Sheila
   • how Sheila changes over the course of the play.

Character Profile — The Inspector

At the end of the play it's not clear who or what the Inspector was. This uncertainty makes a big difference to some of the Birlings, but not to others. "Who was he?" and "Why did he 'call'?" are very different questions...

The Inspector "massively" takes charge

1) The Inspector arrives **unexpectedly**. He just says he's here to ask some questions.

2) He's an **outsider**. He doesn't seem to have much in common with the Birlings.

3) The Inspector leaves after delivering a speech about **social responsibility**. When Gerald finds out that the Inspector is probably a **fake**, the older characters **forget** his speech and try to avoid the blame.

4) He is described as **authoritative** and **imposing**. He's not a big man — but his presence **fills the room**.

Photo: An Inspector Calls, ©2010 Lamb's Players Theatre

Inspector Goole is...

moral: "We don't live alone. We are members of one body"

authoritative: "All in good time"

mysterious: "Was it a hoax?"

an outsider: "The rude way he spoke to Mr Birling and me — it was quite extraordinary!"

The Inspector is the driving force of the play

Think of the Inspector as the **engine** of the play — he keeps things rolling by **asking pushy questions**:

1) He starts it all off with a **summary** of the afternoon's events — "Suicide, of course."

2) He **forces** more information out of people by **bluntly** saying what the other characters try to **skirt around** — e.g. When Gerald's describing how he met Daisy Renton, the Inspector asks "And then you decided to keep her — as your mistress?" But it's **not really a question**. This forces Gerald to admit the **truth**.

3) He also **reveals new information** which **heightens** the **drama**, such as when he drops it into the conversation "that this girl was going to have a child".

The Inspector's 'calling' is pretty ominous

1) The word '**calls**' sounds so **casual** — as if he's just dropping in.

2) '**Calls**' is a **deceptive** word to use about the Inspector. He may appear casual and spontaneous, but in fact he's **single-minded**, **calculating** and is careful to follow "one line of enquiry at a time". If anything, he 'calls' the shots.

3) Another inspector '**calls**' the Birling household on the **telephone** at the end of the play.

4) The title of the play is **echoed** in Edna's words as she announces the arrival of Inspector Goole at the **start of the play** and in the telephone call at the **end of the play**.

Character Profile — The Inspector

His language is emotive and personal

1) Inspector Goole has come to the house to stir things up. He does this with **emotive language**.

2) He describes Eva/Daisy as a "**pretty**" and "**lively**" girl. These **attractive words** make the audience more **sympathetic** towards her.

3) This sympathy is strengthened by the **harsh tone** used to describe her death. He says that she's now lying "**with a burnt-out inside on a slab**".

4) Sheila is "*rather distressed*" by the Inspector's language and says that she "**can't help thinking about this girl — destroying herself**".

© Donald Cooper/Shutterstock

The Inspector uses shock tactics

1) He **answers** his **own questions** if he's not happy with someone's answer — e.g. when Sybil **refuses** to admit there was a committee meeting he says, "**You know very well there was, Mrs Birling.**"

2) He follows up questions with **more questions** until he has pieced together a **confession** — e.g. when Sybil won't say she **convinced** the committee to reject Eva/Daisy's appeal he asks "**Was it or was it not your influence?**"

3) He's **blunt**, "**You're not even sorry now, when you know what happened**", and is prepared to ask **personal questions** — e.g. he asks Gerald "**Were you in love with her?**".

Writer's Technique

Priestley makes the Inspector's language **forceful** and **to the point** — he forces the other characters to **answer** him.

He knows how to make an entrance — and an exit too...

1) The Inspector's timing's **crucial**. Priestley has the Inspector ring the bell just as Arthur says "*a man has to mind his own business*". It's as if Birling's announcement summons the Inspector to prove the **exact opposite**.

For more about entrances and exits see page 48.

2) The Inspector **uses exits** as a **clever tactic**. Leaving Sheila and Gerald alone lets Sheila **interrogate** Gerald and allows the time for **suspicion** to break them apart. This makes it **easier** to get Gerald to confess when the Inspector returns.

3) The Inspector's language gets more **dramatic**, which builds on the **tension** and **emotion** of the final scene. He claims that if the Birlings don't learn their lesson, they will be taught it in "*fire and blood and anguish*".

4) After his last exit there's a sudden **silence** because no one else has been speaking. The audience, like the characters on stage, are left "*staring, subdued and wondering*".

Write about the use of stage directions...

Show that you've paid attention to the whole text by mentioning stage directions. Priestley uses them to describe the Inspector. His imposing voice and "*impression of massiveness*" get everyone under his spell.

Character Profile — The Inspector

Inspector Goole — quite the mystery man. Is he an Inspector? Is he even a man? The audience know by the end that he "definitely wasn't a police inspector at all". But they don't ever find out what he actually was.

Whooo is this Inspector Ghoul?

1) At the end of the play, the audience aren't sure **who** or **what** the Inspector is.

2) He claims he found "<u>a rough sort of diary</u>" kept by Eva/Daisy. But her **identity** isn't certain, and the audience aren't sure she ever **existed** (see p.32-33). So, the diary might be a neat **bluff** to stop anyone asking *him* any questions.

3) Why he has so much knowledge and power is never properly explained. He could be a **ghost**. Or he could represent the **spirit** of a **religious** or **moral** figure — just like in the Medieval morality plays (see p.42).

Writer's Technique

It's a bit of a joke that Inspector Goole's name sounds like 'Ghoul' — a word for 'ghost'. Priestley's put little clues into some of the character's names (see Eva/Daisy on p.8 and p.33).

He's more than a police inspector

1) In a way, he represents the **police** and the **courts** — he's tracking down the truth, like in a murder mystery.

2) Because he's not a police officer, Mr and Mrs Birling don't think he has the **authority** to tell them off.

3) Eric and Sheila realise that his **moral judgement** is just as important as his legal power.

4) Goole has the attitude of a **philosopher** and **social commentator**, and the knowledge of a ghost delivering a prophecy — he warns the Birlings that "<u>the time will soon come</u>" when people like them will be forced to change their ways.

© Alastair Muir/Shutterstock

His authority strengthens his strong moral tone

1) Whatever Goole is, his **unsettling presence** might just be down to **confidence**. He knows how to create an **air of uncertainty** and reel everyone in.

2) He makes sure everyone recognises that he's **in charge**.

3) He takes control and leads the events. They're confused, but Goole **never** is.

4) He "*massively*" interrupts which means that he cuts into the dialogue "*with authority*", e.g. when he tells Birling that Eric can "<u>wait his turn</u>".

5) His **authority** makes people take him **more seriously** and makes everything he says sound more **important**.

TARGET GRADE 8-9

It's significant that Priestley uses a police inspector to judge the Birlings, rather than an overtly 'supernatural' figure. The Inspector unsettles the Birlings because he claims to occupy a position of authority within the Birlings' world. This gives him power because he is a potential threat to their social status.

Writer's Technique

It's worth thinking about how an actor might play the Inspector — maybe with his voice getting **louder and louder** as the play progresses.

Character Profile — The Inspector

The Inspector's from a **different world**

The Inspector doesn't share Arthur Birling's interests or values:

1) The Inspector doesn't play golf and he's **not impressed** by Arthur Birling's public profile as former Alderman and Lord Mayor.

2) He talks about **taboo subjects** like sex and politics.

3) He interrupts _"very sharply"_, repeats questions and pauses in ways which were not the norm in middle-class prewar England. He **doesn't follow etiquette** (normal rules of social behaviour).

For more about etiquette see p.24.

The Inspector is **classless**

1) The Inspector seems to come from **outside** the **class system** that the Birlings live in. This makes him 'classless'.

2) The Inspector doesn't recognise any of the Birlings' ideas about class. He treats **everyone** the **same**.

3) Instead, he says that "We are members of one body" so classes shouldn't **ignore** each other's needs.

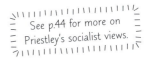

Theme — Social Class

Priestley has set his play in the Birlings' **dining room**. In 1912 only well-off households would have had a dining room — this makes it a **symbol** of the **middle-class lifestyle**.

Priestley uses the Inspector as a **mouthpiece**

See p.44 for more on Priestley's socialist views.

© Pictorial Press Ltd / Alamy Stock Photo

J.B. Priestley

1) The Inspector stands **outside** the **class system** of the Birlings' social world — he is an outsider in the play.

2) But he **doesn't** take a **neutral** position — he's on Eva/Daisy's side and he tells the Birlings what he thinks of them. For example, he doesn't hesitate to tell Mrs Birling that he thinks she "did something terribly wrong".

3) Priestley's **own views** are reflected in the opinions of the Inspector. You could say that the Inspector is Priestley's 'mouthpiece' — Priestley's **voice** in the play.

4) This is most clear during the Inspector's final speech. He's speaking to the Birling family, but it could also be **Priestley's speech** direct to the **play's audience**.

5) The play (and Priestley) has a **strong message** about looking after one another, and it's the Inspector's job to **deliver** it.

KEY QUOTE

"He never seemed like an ordinary police inspector —"

Gosh — what a pickle. Sheila admits that something wasn't right about him from the start, but nobody ever knows who or what Goole is. It does seem like he's been used as Priestley's ventriloquist puppet, though...

Character Profile — Arthur Birling

Arthur Birling's head of the Birling family. He's the boss of his own company. He even plays golf with the big shots. But he's so bothered about money and power that he can't think about anything — or anybody — else.

Arthur Birling seems to be pretty pleased with himself

1) Arthur Birling seems very **confident**. He is head of his **family** and the **boss** of his own business.

2) He likes to be in **control** and he keeps reminding everyone that he's **in charge**, e.g. Birling doesn't want to be told what to do, and "_angrily_" tells the Inspector, "<u>Well — if you don't mind — I'll find out first</u>".

3) Over the course of the play, Birling's authority is **undermined**. The Inspector exposes Birling as an **ambitious**, **anxious** man who'll **ignore** the needs of others to keep up **profits** and a **good reputation**.

© Simon Gough Photography

Birling is...

ambitious: "<u>there's a very good chance of a knighthood</u>"

business-minded: "<u>a hard-headed, practical man of business</u>"

selfish: "<u>a man has to make his own way</u>"

anxious: "<u>there'll be a public scandal — unless we're lucky</u>"

He's a successful and ambitious businessman

1) Birling hints that his company could **merge** with the larger company owned by Gerald's father. He sees his daughter's **marriage** a bit like a **business deal** and hopes it will bring "<u>lower costs and higher prices</u>".

2) Birling thinks he's successful because he's a "<u>hard-headed, practical man of business</u>". He has the same attitude to all areas of his life.

3) He is very **optimistic** about the future. He thinks that strikes won't be a problem for his company and dismisses any fear of **war** as just some "<u>silly little war scares</u>".

Writer's Technique

Priestley uses **dramatic irony** to make Birling's optimism seem **foolish** and **short-sighted** (see page 50). This **undermines** his authority.

He won't accept responsibility for the death of Eva Smith

Theme — Social Responsibility

Birling **dismisses** the idea of **social responsibility**. He calls people like Goole "<u>cranks</u>".

1) Birling finds it difficult to think about other people. He doesn't believe in "<u>community and all that nonsense</u>". He sees other people as "<u>cheap labour</u>".

2) Birling didn't just refuse higher wages for his workers — he **actively** made things worse for them. He **personally** fired the ringleaders of the strike.

3) Birling is **selfish** and **self-centred**. He'd rather pass off the Inspector's visit as a "<u>hoax</u>" or a joke than **face** up to what he's done.

Character Profile — Arthur Birling

Birling likes to be respected — he wants to be in control

1) Birling's a **public figure** in Brumley and obsessed with his **status**. When his good name's threatened he's **terrified** and would "**give thousands**" (a bribe) to avoid scandal.

2) He isn't used to being challenged. The Inspector barely says twenty words before Birling shows "*a touch of impatience*".

3) Birling's family is **falling apart**, and he can do nothing about it. He blames the Inspector for making a "**nasty mess**" of the night's celebrations.

© Studio Canal/Shutterstock

Underneath it all, Birling is an anxious man

Theme — Social Class

Birling's a wealthy businessman, but it was more **prestigious** to come from an "**old county family**" like the Crofts, that had **land**, **inherited wealth** and **titles** (e.g. 'Lord', 'Lady').

1) Birling desperately tries to win the Crofts' **approval** by talking about a knighthood and by getting Gerald's father's favourite port.

2) Birling tries to make himself seem important by drawing attention to his connections with influential people — e.g. he plays **golf** with the Chief Inspector.

3) The Inspector threatens Birling's **middle-class values** — the reputation of his company, his important connections. Birling is **rattled** by this. He has spent his entire life believing that **these things matter**.

TARGET GRADE (8-9)

If you want to take your analysis of Birling's character up a notch, you could write about the conflict between his position as the 'head of the family' and the fact that he's socially inferior to both his wife and the Crofts. Throughout the play, Birling tries to act like he's in charge, but he doesn't always know how to behave. For example, he makes Gerald "*embarrassed*" by tactlessly suggesting that Lady Croft might not approve of Sheila.

Birling uses authoritative language to be in control

Priestley uses **stage directions** and careful **language** choices to help create Birling's character:

1) Priestley writes that Birling should be "*provincial in his speech*", which means he has a **regional accent**. **Accent** and **social class** were closely linked, so it would be clear that Birling was a **middle-class businessman** rather than upper-class.

2) Birling has the most **continuous speech** in the play — he likes to talk and doesn't like being interrupted. When Eric tries to correct him, Birling ignores him, saying "**Just let me finish, Eric**".

3) Birling repeatedly shouts "**Rubbish!**" to **dismiss** what other people have said. But he finishes his own sentences with "**of course**", to make his own claims seem **obvious** and matter-of-fact.

"a man has to mind his own business"

Birling's looking after number one, and he's not going to change. He wants his business to make higher profits, but Priestley uses the character of Birling to show that this profit comes with a high moral cost.

Character Profile — Sybil Birling

Sybil's proud of her reputation and social status. She'll do anything to protect them — they're more important than the happiness of her children. Even when the Inspector's questioning her, she won't back down.

Sybil Birling is proud of her social status

Etiquette
Etiquette is a **set of rules** about social behaviour — what's 'acceptable' and what isn't.

1) Sybil has traditional values. She strictly follows the rules of **etiquette** because a good reputation for being polite will improve her family's **status**. These rules are **more important** to her than **moral rules** — the difference between good and bad.

2) She has a **strong** set of **beliefs** about people's social status, which makes her **prejudiced**.

3) To **preserve** her own status, she's prepared to be **cruel**, such as when she rejects Eva/Daisy's appeal.

© Simon Gough Photography

Sybil is...
traditional: *"When you're married you'll realize..."*
proud: *"I was the only one of you who didn't give in to him"*
prejudiced: *"As if a girl of that sort would ever refuse money!"*
cruel: *"I used my influence to have it refused"*

Sybil is Mr Birling's "social superior"

Sybil Birling is from a family with a **higher social status** than Arthur Birling's family. Even though Arthur's head of the family, Sybil is his *"social superior"*:

1) Sybil tells her husband off for saying the food was good in front of a **guest**. It wasn't **polite** to mention the cook or lower **servants**. **Upper-class families** would not say *"Tell cook from me"*.

2) Sybil's always reminding her family to have **better manners** — e.g. she tells Sheila off for using **slang**.

3) Sybil won't let anyone **boss** her around. She warns the Inspector, *"You have no power to make me change my mind"*.

© Everett Collection Inc /Alamy Stock Photo

Sybil lives by strict standards

1) Sybil's social standards make her prejudiced against people from a **lower class**. She thinks that they have **lower standards** and can't imagine her son being involved with women *"of that sort"*.

2) It's her 'standards' that make her walk **straight into** the Inspector's trap when he asks her who **she blames** for Eva/Daisy's suicide.

3) Even though it was Sybil herself who **refused** to help Eva/Daisy when she **most needed it**, she **blames** the father of the unborn child.

4) Without realising it, she condemns her own son and demands that he should be **made to pay**, and to **confess publicly**.

Character Profile — Sybil Birling

Sybil supports charity — but she's not very charitable

1) Mrs Birling is involved with the Brumley Women's Charity Organisation which she says only supports "deserving cases".

2) This gives Mrs Birling the authority to decide who's "deserving" and who's not.

3) She uses her "influence" (social status) to convince the other members of the board to reject Eva/Daisy's appeal because she's offended by the young woman using the Birling name.

4) She's outraged that Eva/Daisy would pretend to have the "fine feelings" of a higher social class, but Mrs Birling is unfeeling towards the women who make appeals to her.

Theme — Social Responsibility

The word "deserving" was traditionally used to distinguish between the poor who physically can't help themselves and the 'undeserving' who some people felt shouldn't be helped.

Mrs Birling doesn't change

© Simon Gough Photography

1) Mrs Birling is self-centred. She hasn't noticed her own son's alcoholism and dismisses her daughter's worries that Gerald lost interest last summer.

2) She won't accept responsibility for her actions, and claims that she did the right thing — "I accept no blame for it at all".

3) She doesn't learn from the Inspector's message. She only regrets not having "asked him a few questions" — she wants to be in control.

Stage directions show Mrs Birling has her mind made up

Even when her language is polite, her tone is severe and superior:

1) The stage directions say that Mrs Birling answers "haughtily", "very sharply" and "bitterly".

2) In Act Three, Mrs Birling repeatedly tells everyone that she'd already guessed it was a hoax. The script says that she "triumphantly" tells everyone she knew it all along. It's more important to her that she comes out on top, than that her actions could have caused a girl's suicide.

3) In the final moments of the play, Mrs Birling is "smiling" and telling everyone to feel as "amused" as she is by the evening's events. These words suggest she has already put it all behind her.

EXAM TIP

Remember to talk about Sybil's social prejudices...

Mentioning Sybil's social prejudices will help you explain why she acts the way she does. She doesn't think Eva/Daisy's important as she's socially inferior. And at the end of the play, Sybil hasn't changed at all.

Character Profile — Sheila Birling

Sheila's not heard the old saying 'start as you mean to go on' — at the beginning of the play she seems childish and petty, but later reveals herself as thoughtful, sensitive and sharp. By the end, Sheila wants to start again...

Sheila seems to be different from the rest of her family

1) Sheila's **quick-witted** and **strong-minded**. She hands Gerald's ring back when she finds out he's been unfaithful and is wise enough to suspect that Eric might be the father of Eva/Daisy's child.

2) However, Sheila was **more selfish** the year before. She **abused her status** as a wealthy customer at Milwards when she insisted they **dismiss Eva/Daisy**.

3) Sheila is now seen to be **sensitive** and **moral**. By the end of the play, Sheila has **changed for good**.

Sheila is...

strong-minded: "I don't believe I will. So you be careful."

sharp: "he's giving us the rope — so that we'll hang ourselves"

selfish: "you used the power you had [...] to punish the girl"

moral: "But these girls aren't cheap labour — they're *people*"

Sheila's language makes her seem childish at first...

1) The stage directions say she's "*very pleased with life and rather excited*".

2) She uses slang expressions like "*squiffy*" which remind the audience that Sheila belongs to a **younger generation**.

3) When she gets the ring she's very **excited**, and looks to her mother for **approval** when she says "Look — Mummy — isn't it a beauty?"

4) She **jokes** with Gerald, but the stage directions say that she's "*half serious, half playful*". Her childishness might be a way to hide "*serious*" concerns about her relationship with Gerald.

Writer's Technique

Priestley gives Sheila lots of **witty lines** to make her appear sharp. Sheila's **wit** lets her **undermine** the **authority** of the others as she makes jokes at their expense.

...but Sheila's more mature than the audience first think

Sheila behaves childishly at the beginning, but what she **learns** over the evening makes her feel she has to be herself and break away from her parents.

1) She has **wise** instincts — she sees what the Inspector is doing, and knew Gerald's absence was **suspicious**.

2) She's **not naive** — she knows men use **prostitutes** and knows about **dirty old men** like Alderman Meggarty.

3) As the Inspector says, she "isn't living on the moon", and as she says to her father, "I'm not a child."

Character Profile — Sheila Birling

Sheila has moral standards

1) Sheila acknowledges she used her *"power"* to *"punish"* Eva Smith, but she regrets her actions and is eager to **learn** from the **consequences**.

2) Priestley uses her as a moral judge at the end of the play — she says *"probably between us we killed her"*. The others don't get as far as admitting that.

3) She tells Gerald she respects him more for being *"honest"*. She also knows the family must **stop** these *"silly pretences"*. Priestley uses Sheila to show there's **hope** for **change** in the new generation.

> **Theme — Learning about Life**
>
> Priestley makes Sheila seem young and **childish** at first. It makes her involvement in Eva/Daisy's downfall seem like the result of **immaturity**. This makes it **easier to forgive** her.

The Inspector's revelations change her for good

1) Before Gerald leaves, she **hands back** the engagement ring, saying that they are **changed people** — *"You and I aren't the same people who sat down to dinner here."*

2) After the Inspector goes, her parents want everything to return to the **way it was**. Sheila and Eric are the only ones who see that they all **have to change**.

3) Out of **all** the characters in the play Sheila's the one who changes the **most**.

> **TARGET GRADE 8-9**
>
> Sheila's final line adds some ambiguity to how the audience sees her character. When Gerald offers her the ring back, she replies, "It's too soon. I must think." Her hesitation shows that she's been affected by the Inspector's message — she needs to think about the kind of life she wants to lead. But she leaves open the possibility of taking Gerald back and returning to normal — this could hint that even Sheila might eventually forget the Inspector's lesson.

Sheila becomes a bit like the Inspector herself

It's not surprising that Sheila takes the Inspector's **side** in a lot of this, and even seems to **help** the Inspector's investigations. They're both after the **truth**. She adopts some of the Inspector's techniques:

1) She asks Gerald as many **questions** as the Inspector does.

2) She **reveals** Eric's **drinking problem** to her mother.

3) She **contradicts** and **undermines** her parents, like the Inspector does. When she's giving the ring back to Gerald she tells her father, *"Don't interfere"*.

4) She **shocks** Eric by telling him that his mother **refused** to **help** Eva/Daisy. The Inspector **moves** the discussion on quickly by suddenly **startling** the listeners, and Sheila does the same.

© Chesil Theatre Winchester

Sheila sees that the Inspector **attacks** the others' confidence by asking questions. He does this to break down the *"wall"* which they've put between **themselves** and the girl — Sheila wants to do the same.

EXAM TIP

Write about how Sheila's character develops...

Sheila offers hope to the audience — she grows up by the end of the play and realises she needs to change her priorities. Explain in your essay that she allows the Inspector's story to affect and change her.

Character Profile — Eric Birling

Eric is a troubled soul. He has turned away from his family and taken up drinking. But no one seems to notice, or at least they think it's more polite to not mention it. So, instead, Eric's friendless and stuck.

Eric Birling is a **troublesome** son

1) Eric's **isolated** from the rest of his family. He says that **no one understands** him and he doesn't feel as if he can talk to any of them.

2) Eric apparently forced himself on Eva/Daisy while he was **drunk** and got her **pregnant**. He was so drunk he didn't even remember it happening.

3) Eric deeply **regrets** his actions — by the end of the play he says he'll **never forget** what he has learnt.

© Simon Gough Photography

Eric is...

irresponsible: "**I didn't even remember — that's the hellish thing**"

unloved: "**You don't understand anything. You never did.**"

sensitive: "**My God — I'm not likely to forget**"

an alcoholic: "**I was in that state when a chap easily turns nasty**"

Priestley **drops hints** that Eric isn't all right

1) Priestley's stage directions say that Eric is *"**not quite at ease**"*. He's described as being *"**half shy**"* and *"**half assertive**"*.

2) He **interrupts** Sheila and Gerald when he *"**suddenly guffaws**"*, but says he doesn't know why he's laughing. He finds things his family say funny, even when there's **no joke**.

3) When Gerald says, *"**Unless Eric's been up to something,**"* Eric acts **suspiciously** and **seriously** — *"**I don't think it's very funny,**"* he says *"**still uneasy**"*, and also answers *"**defiantly**"*.

Writer's Technique

Priestley uses Eric's **odd behaviour** to hint that his secrets will **later disrupt** and threaten the Birlings' whole **way of life**.

Eric's been **hiding** some **dirty secrets**

Eric's **drunkenness** and **bad behaviour** represent the **dark side** of family life.

1) He's a **heavy drinker**, and has been for a while. You can see his *"**familiarity with quick heavy drinking**"* in the way he pours his whisky in Act Three. The rest of the family sees it too.

2) He got a prostitute **pregnant** — his first encounter with Eva/Daisy results in her getting **pregnant** and there's a suggestion that he **forced** himself on her.

3) He has **stolen money** from his father's business to support her.

© Simon Gough Photography

These secrets are **potential dynamite** — if they got out and became public gossip, then Birling's knighthood, Sheila's marriage and the **whole family's reputation** could be blown sky high.

Character Profile — Eric Birling

Eric's **not** the **only** one...

1) Eric meets Eva/Daisy at the stalls bar, which is exactly where **Gerald** met her, when he was looking for **prostitutes**.

2) Birling's "**respectable friends**" go to the stalls bar to find women. The Alderman, Meggarty, even assaults young women in the town hall. They're all behaving **badly**. But no one says **anything**.

3) It's a pretty **murky world** that these 'respectable' men inhabit. The play suggests Eric's behaviour is normal for a **middle-class man**.

Two finely dressed upper-class (not always) gentlemen.

... but he's the only one to have **serious consequences**

1) Eric's behaviour was **not unusual** — lots of men were doing the same... just in **secret**. Eric **lacks self-control** so his secret gets out.

2) His parents don't want a **scandal**. They don't care about him as much as they care about what **other people** will think of them.

3) Eric's laugh **interrupts** the **polite conversation** earlier in the play. It's the same when his behaviour **disrupts** the polite middle-class **illusion** of **respectability**. They're all **keeping up appearances** — but Eric's making it **obvious** that there's something murky underneath.

Theme — Judgement

Gerald treats Eva/Daisy as his "**mistress**" and ends the affair — his **reputation** is **not damaged**. But Eric **drunkenly** gets Eva/Daisy **pregnant**, **steals** money for her and brings a **scandal** on his family.

Eric is a **villain** and a **victim**

Theme — Family Life

Birling seems **disappointed** in his son, and gets on better with Gerald. This must be a **crushing blow** for Eric.

1) Eric feels **isolated** and **unsupported** — he's had to find comfort elsewhere.

2) He shouts at his mother — "**You don't understand anything. You never did. You never even tried —**" and perhaps he's right. But he's really **yelling**. It might be the **angriest moment** in the play.

3) He's the obvious villain of the piece, but he accepts **responsibility** for what he did — "**the fact remains that I did what I did**". He criticises his parents for **pretending nothing's happened** — "**You lot may be letting yourselves out nicely**".

KEY QUOTE

"the fact remains that I did what I did."

At first, it seems clear that Eric has the lowest morals of all the characters. But then he regrets his mistakes and learns from them. He comes the furthest — the audience start to see him in a more sympathetic light.

Character Profile — Gerald Croft

Gerald's the son-in-law Mr Birling dreamt of. He's the son of the competition, Crofts Limited.
His mother's a Lady. He's respectable. So, apart from the secret mistress, he's spot on.

Gerald Croft is an eligible bachelor

1) At the start, Gerald seems like a good catch. He **gets on well** with Mr Birling and **impresses** Sybil Birling.

2) But then it turns out Gerald's been **lying** — he confesses that he had a fling with Daisy Renton last summer. Sheila hands his engagement ring back.

3) Gerald leads the Birlings to realise that Inspector Goole was not a police officer, and that there was no suicide recorded at the hospital. He **sides** with Mr Birling, focusing on how to protect their **reputation**.

Photo: An Inspector Calls, ©2010 Lamb's Players Theatre

Gerald is...

respectable: "<u>the easy well-bred young man-about-town</u>"

upper-class: "<u>landed people and so forth</u>"

a liar: "<u>I wasn't telling you a complete lie</u>"

traditional: "<u>I should say so!</u>" (Gerald agreeing with Birling)

Gerald's got a rosy future ahead of him...

Gerald's got a lot going for him. He's **handsome**, **wealthy**, **about thirty** — a respectable man-about-town.

1) He's from an **old county family** — unlike the Birlings. That makes him their **social superior**.

2) Gerald works for 'Crofts Limited'. This is his father's firm, and is older and bigger than 'Birling and Company' — the two companies are "<u>friendly rivals</u>". He'll probably take it over when his father retires.

3) He's relaxed and **comfortable** in this company (unlike Eric), and shares jokes with Birling.

... but it's a future that looks an awful lot like Birling's

Gerald's like a **younger** version of Arthur Birling.
He's used to and comfortable with being in control.

1) Gerald agrees with Birling on **politics** and **women** and **laughs** at his **joke** about getting into trouble.

2) He **supports** Arthur's sacking of Eva Smith — "<u>You couldn't have done anything else.</u>"

3) He's **business-minded** and is committed to his work in the same way that Arthur Birling is.

4) He and Arthur are the ones who are determined to take **action** at the end to find out whether the Inspector or the girl were real.

Theme — Young and Old

If it wasn't for Gerald, it'd be easy to say that Mr and Mrs Birling are **selfish** and **unchanging** because they're **too old**. But Gerald's character shows that **younger people** can be just as **selfish** and **old-fashioned**.

Character Profile — Gerald Croft

Gerald's language shows he doesn't feel sorry for his actions

Priestley makes Gerald sound **less passionate** than Sheila. Gerald can **distance** himself from the tragedy.

© Simon Gough Photography

1) He's the **first character** to use the word "**hoax**" — he's very keen to prove the Inspector was a **fake** and clear everyone's names.

2) At the end of the play, he says "<u>Everything's all right now, Sheila</u>" to comfort her. He doesn't seem to have learnt any lessons.

He thinks he's done nothing wrong

Theme — Social Class

Gerald might have made Eva/Daisy **happy** for a time, but he still **treated her badly** because of her **social status**. He kept her as a mistress for his own **pleasure** and discarded her when it suited him.

1) Gerald says that Eva/Daisy "<u>didn't blame me at all</u>". Perhaps the audience **don't blame Gerald** much at first because **Eva/Daisy didn't**.

2) The Inspector isn't too harsh on him because Gerald "<u>had some affection for her and made her happy for a time</u>". Gerald had some **positive effects** on Eva/Daisy's life.

3) But then he **left her** and went off on a business trip. He effectively made her **homeless**.

Gerald's not simply bad or good

This is a **difficult** one. Priestley's made it hard to see Gerald as simply good or bad. He's a complex character.

1) Gerald is confident but he's also **stubborn** — he doesn't learn much about himself over the course of the play. The Inspector points out Gerald's **hypocrisy**:

- The Inspector asks Gerald whether he thinks "<u>young women ought to be protected against unpleasant and disturbing things</u>". Gerald says yes, thinking of Sheila.

- **But** it's people like Gerald who are **doing** the unpleasant and disturbing things to women like Eva/Daisy — he uses her and then **discards** her. This applies just as much to Mr Birling and **other men** like him who have the **same attitudes**.

2) Gerald has the ability to **separate** his **public**, **respectable image** from secret, **private acts** — something Eric doesn't get the hang of.

TARGET GRADE 8-9

Whereas Priestley uses dramatic irony to make Mr and Mrs Birling appear foolish and overconfident, Gerald is often portrayed as a more perceptive character. For example, in Act Two, Gerald attempts to warn Mrs Birling against intimidating the Inspector, since he knows it will only make things worse. This could make the audience judge Gerald more harshly, because he has the intelligence to understand the Inspector's point but chooses to ignore it.

 KEY QUOTE

"Everything's all right now, Sheila."

Gerald was upset when he learnt that Eva/Daisy was dead — but he's gotten over it already. He won't let a fake inspector play a prank on him. Not when he's got a reputation to maintain, and Sheila to win back.

Character Profile — Eva Smith / Daisy Renton

Who was Eva Smith? No idea. Were Eva Smith and Daisy Renton the same person? Was she even real?
No idea. What matters most is what Eva/Daisy represents, and what she means to the Birlings.

Who was Eva Smith?

1) Eva Smith was one of Arthur Birling's employees, who was **sacked** for **protesting** against **lower wages**.
   This dismissal is the first in a **chain of events** that sees the Birling family tied up in Eva Smith's death.

2) According to the Inspector, Eva Smith changes her name to Daisy Renton and
   becomes a **prostitute**, which is how she meets Gerald and Eric.

3) The **real identity** of Eva/Daisy is **never revealed**. She could be the **same person**, or **different people** who
   are treated as **the same** by the Birling family. They see one working-class girl as being the same as another.

©iStock.com/ianmcdonnell

Eva/Daisy is...

attractive: "**young and fresh and charming**"

honourable: "**she didn't want to take any more money
from him**"

working-class: "**Girls of that class**", "**a girl of that sort**"

a prostitute: "**There was some woman who wanted her to
go there**"

The Birlings take away all of Eva/Daisy's sources of income

1) **Factory worker** at Birling and Company — she was a
   good worker but Birling sacked her for **speaking up**.
   According to Birling, "**she had to go.**"

2) **Shop assistant** at Milwards — Sheila got her
   sacked out of **jealousy** for Eva/Daisy's good looks.

3) **Prostitute** and **mistress** to Gerald — he rescued her from
   the life of a **prostitute** but **dropped** her when it **suited** him.

4) **Prostitute** — she can't **make a living** this way after Eric forced
   her to have sex and got her **pregnant** while he was drunk.

Theme — Social Class

Eva/Daisy lost **all** these
forms of **support** because
other people used their
power to move her on or
have sex with her. Each of
them felt **superior** to Eva
because of their social class.

She never sought revenge, so the Inspector does it for her

1) Priestley has made Eva/Daisy a **silent**, **offstage** character, so in the play
   she represents the **silent**, **invisible** and **powerless** members of **society**.

2) Maybe Eva/Daisy didn't feel that she had the **power** to make life
   difficult for people like Birling who "**made her pay a heavy price**"
   for challenging his authority. She was **trapped** by her situation.

3) Inspector Goole **speaks** for Eva/Daisy and uses her as a **symbol**
   of the powerless working class to teach the Birlings about **social
   responsibility** and to make them realise their **mistakes**.

Theme — Social Class

Some productions of
An Inspector Calls put
Eva/Daisy **on stage**,
sometimes as a **ghost**.

Character Profile — Eva Smith / Daisy Renton

Were Eva Smith and Daisy Renton the same person?

1) Gerald claims there were lots of **different** girls — "<u>We've no proof it was the same photograph and therefore no proof it was the same girl.</u>"

2) But Gerald also says that Daisy Renton told him about having to leave a "<u>job in one of the works here</u>" after a strike and "<u>something about the shop too</u>" — so Eva Smith **must** be Daisy Renton. But...

Photo: An Inspector Calls, ©2010 Lamb's Players Theatre

- The **phone call** at the end of the play confuses everything. Has Eva/Daisy just taken her own life? Was the Inspector a **ghost** come to tell the **future**?

- Or is this a phone call about a **different** girl? The Inspector warned that everyone's lives are "<u>intertwined</u>", so the Birlings don't know how many lives they have affected.

- Priestley makes sure that, even if you think you've sussed it, that phone call **breaks up** the girl's **identity** again.

Eva Smith is a sort of everyman

The identity of Eva Smith is a kind of jigsaw portrait of an **ordinary working-class girl**, only you don't know if the pieces fit.

© Bridgeman Images

1) Take her first name. "<u>Eva</u>" — a bit like **Eve**, the first woman (so the Bible says) and **symbolic** of all women.

2) Take her second name — Smith. It's a very **common** last name, and it's from the word for a **tradesman**.

3) **That's it** — Eva Smith represents "<u>millions and millions and millions</u>" of **ordinary, working-class women**.

Eva Smith is central to the play's message

1) The Inspector says that there are "<u>millions of Eva Smiths and John Smiths still left</u>" and that their chances of happiness are "<u>intertwined with our lives</u>".

2) This is the key point — the Inspector is telling the Birlings, and the audience, to behave **responsibly** towards others.

3) So, although the focus of the **drama** is the group of five people sitting around the dining table at the beginning, the focus of the **play** is the life and death of an **unidentified** and **unseen** woman. If they all met **different** girls, it doesn't matter. Eva/Daisy is a **mix** of all the people they've ever **treated badly**.

EXAM TIP

Think about the message that Eva/Daisy conveys...

It's useful to say that Priestley uses Eva/Daisy as a way to show his audience how everyone is responsible for one another. He wanted people to realise that everything they do could affect someone else.

Practice Questions

Congratulations — that's another section done. As a special reward for your hard work, here's a trophy and a huge cake. Oh no, sorry, it's two pages of practice questions. Well, don't spend too long on these quick and in-depth questions — just use them to warm up for the next page. What a treat.

Quick Questions

1) How did each of the Birlings affect the life of Eva/Daisy?

2) Give two examples of how the Inspector manages to unsettle Mr Birling.

For even more practice, try the *An Inspector Calls* Sudden Fail Quiz — just scan this QR code!

Inspector Quiz

3) Summarise the message of the Inspector's speech in one sentence.

4) Find three stage directions that show how the Inspector is supposed to talk and look.

5) Give an example of how Arthur tries to impress the Inspector.

6) Name three ways in which Sybil and Sheila are different from each other.

7) In one sentence, describe how Sheila comes across at the beginning of the play.

8) Find a quote to show that Eric regrets his actions.

9) Give two reasons why Gerald Croft is seen to be socially superior to the Birlings.

10) Which character first suggests that the photograph is key to finding out Eva/Daisy's true identity? What does this character say about the photograph?

In-depth Questions

1) Who or what is the Inspector? Do you think that Priestley wants us to know?

2) At the start of the play, Birling is in control. When and how do you think the balance of power shifts from Birling to the Inspector?

3) If you were in charge of costume design for *An Inspector Calls*, how would you dress Mr Birling and the Inspector? You can sketch out an idea or write a paragraph explaining why you chose these costumes.

4) Do you think Sheila and Gerald should get married? Why do you think this?

5) Do you think Mrs Birling learns anything from the Inspector's visit? Use quotations from the text to back up your answer.

6) Both Eric and Gerald have relationships with Eva/Daisy. What do you feel about the way each man behaves towards her?

7) For much of the play, the younger generation (Sheila and Eric) hold different views from the older generation (Mr and Mrs Birling). Whose views does Gerald share? Find some quotations to back up your answer.

8) Explain the symbolism of Eva Smith's name and how this fits in with her role in the play.

Practice Questions

Now it's time for the biggies. Use all your knowledge and skill to answer these questions.

Target Grade 8-9

1) 'The Inspector's authority over the Birlings comes from the sense that he is all-knowing.' How far do you agree with this statement?

2) 'Eric should be seen as more of a victim than a villain.' Do you agree with this statement? Give evidence from the play to support your answer.

3) Do you think Gerald cared about Eva/Daisy, or was he just shocked that someone he knew died in such a horrible way? Find evidence from the text to support your opinion.

4) The play ends with a telephone call. How might the audience's understanding of the title *An Inspector Calls* change between the Inspector's arrival and the end of the play?

Exam-style Questions

1) Write about how Priestley presents the character of Eva Smith/Daisy Renton.
   Think about:
   • how the other characters describe her
   • why her character is important in the play.

2) 'The Birling family are presented as a close and happy family at the beginning of the play, but are left broken by the end.'
   How far do you agree with this assessment of the presentation of the Birling family?

3) **Gerald: Everything's all right now, Sheila. [*Holds up the ring.*] What about this ring?**
   How does Priestley present the changing relationship between Sheila and Gerald during the play?

4) How does Priestley use the character of the Inspector to explore the play's key messages?
   Think about:
   • what the Inspector's function is in the play
   • how Priestley presents the Inspector.

5) How does Priestley present the character of Sybil Birling to the audience during the play?
   Think about:
   • how Sybil interacts with other characters
   • how Priestley presents her character.

6) Look at Act Three, from the beginning of the act to where Mr Birling says "**I understand a lot of things now I didn't understand before.**"
   With reference to this passage and the play as a whole, write about Eric's relationship with Mr Birling.

7) 'Priestley suggests the Birlings are flawed but have the potential to change.' How far do you agree?

Section Three — Context and Themes

Britain in 1912 and 1945

An Inspector Calls is set near the beginning of the 20th century. Priestley wrote it in the 1940s. You're reading it now in the 21st century. How things have changed...

In 1912 Britain was very different from how it is now

1) British society was firmly **divided** along **class** lines. Those with the **most money** had the **most power**. The **Labour Party** was formed in 1906 to represent the **interests** of the working class.

2) Only men who owned **property** could vote. **Women** weren't allowed to **vote** in national elections at all. Women's lives were far **more controlled** by their families and husbands than today.

3) There was not as much government help for people in need as there is today. This is why **charities** like the "Brumley Women's Charity Organization" were so **important**.

The 1912 National Miners' Strike — over a million workers across Britain campaigned for fairer wages for miners. At the time it was the largest strike in Britain.

© Mary Evans / Robert Hunt Collection

Britain was heading towards the First World War...

- There was a dangerous level of **tension** between the big European countries in 1912, which resulted in the First World War (1914-1918). This was a **terrible conflict** which cost **millions of lives**.

- After the war many British people **questioned** the **leadership** given by the **upper classes** during the war.

Things had changed by 1945 — but there were still big problems

1) Britain was still divided by class, but by 1928 all **men** and **women** over **21** got the **vote**, which meant **power** was shared out more **evenly**.

2) There were still conflicts between business owners and workers, such as the 1926 **General Strike** which saw many important **industries** grind to a halt.

3) From 1930 a **global economic slump** known as the **Depression** hit many British industries. There was a big increase in **unemployment** and many workers faced terrible **poverty**.

Priestley wrote the play during the Second World War

- **Millions** of people from all classes had **fought** for Britain during the Second World War (1939-1945). After the war people wanted to work out how to make a better **society**.

- The world wars made people **question** Britain's **social structure**. **Socialism** and other **left-wing** ideas, which call for the more equal sharing out of wealth and power, became more **popular**. These views are represented in the play by **the Inspector**, who argues that people should be "responsible for each other".

- The **Labour Party** won the 1945 General Election by a landslide. In government they focused on improving the **welfare system** to look after the needs of the **poorest** in British society, e.g. the NHS was started in 1948.

Right-wing ideas favour private ownership and wealth.

EXAM TIP

Talk about why Priestley set the play when he did...

Mention that a lot changed in British society between 1912 and 1945. Priestley set the play at the start of the 20th century to show that things had improved, but he also highlights that many things had not.

Family Life

At the start, Gerald thinks that the Birlings seem to be "a nice well-behaved family". But Gerald, and the audience, are yet to find out about the murky secrets lurking behind their polite and polished behaviour.

There were expectations of middle-class families in 1912

1) Family members were expected to **know their role**, and be **content** with their **position** — the parents were **in charge** of the family, and the children were expected to be **obedient** and **unquestioning**.

2) '**Gender roles**' (how men and women are supposed to behave) were well **defined** for the **wealthy middle class**:

Men were expected to:
- Work to **support** their '**perfect**' family.
- **Protect women** — especially their wives and daughters — from "**unpleasant and disturbing things**".

Women were expected to:
- **Marry** into money so they didn't have to work.
- Plan **parties**, visit **friends** and **have children**. They didn't do jobs like **washing**, **cooking** or **cleaning**.

3) However, **working-class** families, and especially working-class **women**, had very different roles. Many had **jobs** in factories or worked as servants.

The Birling family seems fairly normal...

1) The Birlings want everyone to **believe** they're the **perfect family**.

2) The **gender roles** are clearly **defined** — the ladies 'withdraw' to let the men talk about 'male' stuff.

3) But there's **tension** bubbling just under the surface:

- Mrs Birling keeps correcting her family's **social mistakes**.
- Eric laughs out of turn and acts **oddly**.
- Sheila **teases** Gerald half playfully, but also "**half serious**", about last summer.

Photo: An Inspector Calls, ©2010 Lamb's Players Theatre

... but something's not right

1) The clear **hierarchy** at the beginning is **destroyed** by the Inspector's arrival.

A hierarchy is a way of ranking people according to status or authority.

2) Without their parents' influence, Sheila and Eric can **think for themselves**:

- Sheila doesn't know whether she'll marry Gerald any more. She needs time to decide for herself.

- Eric says his mother doesn't "**understand anything**" and that Birling's "**not the kind of father a chap could go to**" for help.

- The family is in a **mess**, and Sheila and Eric **refuse** to "**go on behaving just as we did**". They don't want to **pretend** any more. The parents no longer have any **authority** over their children.

KEY QUOTE

"You seem to be a nice well-behaved family —"

The Birling family is held together by lies, and when the truth's revealed they fall apart. And it's not pretty. There's hatred, envy, theft, prostitutes, and even being responsible for the death of your own grandchild...

Social Class

Social class is really important in *An Inspector Calls*. Class influences the Birlings' behaviour and causes them to treat people differently. The class system had existed for a long time and Priestley didn't agree with it.

Class drives the plot and shapes the characters

Photo: An Inspector Calls, ©2010 Lamb's Players Theatre

1) Priestley **designed** the characters to put across his **message** that all people "are members of one body".

2) The message is about **social responsibility**, so class plays a **central part** in the plot.

3) The characters in the play **represent** the classes — and Priestley challenges their **views** and **behaviour** in order to challenge the **class hierarchy**.

There was a clear class structure in the early 20th century

Many things contributed to what class you were in, but most of it came down to **money** — those who had it, and those who didn't. There were **three** main classes:

Working Class	Middle Class	Upper Class
Had all the **hardest jobs** and **little money**.	**Owned** factories or were **professionals** (like lawyers). Had **plenty of money** and **control**.	**Inherited** loads of land and money. Were often **Lords** and **Ladies**.

Eva/Daisy	The Birlings	Gerald
She **struggles** through life, doing tough jobs, only just earning enough to **survive**.	The Birlings are **wealthy**, own a **business** and are able to live very **comfortably**.	Gerald's mother's family are "landed people", so Gerald's family is socially '**better**' than Arthur's. **Inherited money** had a higher status than trade.

The class system meant the lower classes struggled

1) The class system could make life **difficult** for those lower down — it would have been hard for people like Eva/Daisy to help themselves if they were in **trouble**.

2) Priestley portrays the upper classes as having a **limited** sense of **social responsibility** for those less well off. They either:

   DIDN'T KNOW   OR   DIDN'T WANT TO KNOW   OR   DIDN'T CARE

3) Mrs Birling claims not to recognise Eva/Daisy's photo. For her, Eva/Daisy has **no identity**.

4) Priestley suggested that the higher classes didn't question the class system as it **worked** for them. This is the same reason why they also **overlooked** problems of **alcoholism** and **womanising** — it was easier to ignore unpleasant things than to deal with them.

5) The Inspector tells the Birlings that they must **accept** that everyone should take **responsibility** for each other, or it'll all end in "fire", "blood" and "anguish".

Social Class

The Birlings think class is all that matters

1) Birling's biggest **concern** about Eva's death is that he won't get his knighthood because there will be a "**public scandal**".

2) Birling thinks his positions of **authority** make him more **important**. He'd been **Lord Mayor** and an **Alderman** (Council member) for many years, and he's now a **magistrate** who sits in courts and dishes out justice.

3) He uses Gerald to **promote** his social class — he asks him to hint to his parents that he's expecting a knighthood, and he's also very pleased that his daughter is marrying into a **higher class**.

4) Sybil Birling is a leading member of the Brumley **Women's Charity Organisation**. This group's **supposed** to give money to desperate women, but Mrs Birling's only involved for the social **status**.

> **Theme — Judgement**
>
> It's ironic that Birling **passes judgement** on others when he's acted so **immorally**.

Priestley thought class shouldn't matter

1) Priestley uses the play to **reveal** the **unfairness** of the class system — he uses the Birlings as exaggerated **caricatures** of all the **bad qualities** he thought the ruling classes had.

2) The play isn't just about **one family's scandal**. It shows how Priestley saw **society**. Priestley presents the Birlings' arrogant behaviour and selfish attitudes as **common** to the middle classes.

3) Priestley presents the working class as **victims** of the **class system** — although Eva/Daisy's story is **unique**, the miseries she suffered were **common** to "**millions and millions**" of people. Eva Smith could have been **anyone**.

© Jimmy Sime/Stringer/Hulton Archive/Getty Images

How people act isn't just about class

1) Eva/Daisy is expected to have **low morals** — Mrs Birling describes her as "**not a good case**". Despite this, Eva/Daisy **refuses** to accept stolen money even when she's desperate.

2) The Birlings think that **class** is all that matters, but Priestley is trying to present the **opposite view**. He suggests that class only **clouds** people's **judgements**, and people should be judged by **what they do**, not by what class they happen to be in.

3) By presenting Sheila and Eric as having **changed** at the end of the play, **turning against** the views of their own class, Priestley's saying that class isn't all that matters — individuals can **break out** and choose to act differently.

> **TARGET GRADE 8-9**
>
> Think about the kind of people who might have watched Priestley's play when it was first performed. In 1940s London, going to the theatre was mostly a middle-class activity, so the attitudes of the Birlings may have seemed familiar to some audiences. Priestley's presentation of Eva/Daisy as more honourable than the upper and middle classes might have caused some audience members to question their own prejudices.

EXAM TIP

Talk about how the Inspector doesn't have a class...

The Inspector doesn't clearly fit into the class structure, and he thinks everyone should be treated equally. You could write about how he challenges attitudes about class, and makes Sheila and Eric want to change.

Young and Old

The Inspector, and his story about Eva Smith/Daisy Renton, causes a rift between the old traditionalists and the young idealists. One side wants nothing to do with the story — the other feels like it's their job to rewrite it.

The older generation are old-fashioned

1) Priestley presents Arthur and Sybil Birling as having very **traditional views** — they think that they **know best**, that children should be **seen and not heard**, and they don't like their authority to be **challenged**.

2) They represent the views of the **ruling class**. This means they feel **superior** to people like Eva/Daisy, who is written off by Mrs Birling as a girl _"of that class"_.

3) By **questioning** their old-fashioned **personal views**, Priestley also questions their **obsession** with **social class** — he's suggesting that the whole class system is **out of touch** and needs to be **reformed**.

The younger generation are different

1) Some are **ambitious**, **determined** and **motivated** — Eva/Daisy _"had a lot to say — far too much"_. Her **courage** is the main reason Birling sacked her.

2) The younger generation are shown as **challenging** the **authority** of their elders. This **threatens** Birling, who tells them they'd _"better keep quiet"_.

3) Because the younger generation **learn** their lesson, there's **a chance** for an **equal** and **fairer** society in the future.

> **Theme — Learning**
> Eric and Sheila learn that they are **responsible** for their **actions** and that their **decisions** affect **other people**.

Eric at the end is standing around as if he wants **nothing** to do with his parents. Sheila stands by him. By the end of the play they're no longer **controlled** by their parents.

Gerald's the oldest young man around

1) Gerald's closer to Sheila and Eric's age than he is to Mr and Mrs Birling's, but he's a young man who's already **old** in his **attitudes**. He's a **younger version** of Arthur — shallow and stubborn:

- His **marriage** to Sheila is for business reasons.
- He **agrees** with **Birling** that Eva/Daisy had to be **fired**.

Photo: An Inspector Calls, ©2010 Lamb's Players Theatre

2) He **doesn't learn anything**:

- When he's found out to have **ditched** Eva/Daisy, he doesn't seem to feel **guilty**.
- At the end, he thinks his **engagement's** back on: _"Everything's all right now, Sheila."_

3) The fact that Gerald is of the younger generation but remains **unchanged** suggests that a more caring future **isn't inevitable** — people can **choose** whether to **change** or not. Priestley is also making a criticism of the **upper classes**, that they're **set in their ways** and therefore unlikely to change.

"the famous younger generation who know it all."

Although Birling's being sarcastic, Priestley shows that the only characters who really listen to the Inspector's message are Sheila and Eric. Mr and Mrs Birling aren't as willing to change or learn from their mistakes.

Men and Women

In 1912, men and women had different roles in the family and society — they led very different lives from each other. Priestley is asking his audience to think about how people are treated differently because of their gender.

The women and men start out as stereotypes

A **stereotype** is an **idea** you might have about people before you really know them. It's usually based on things like their sex, age and class.

WOMEN

1) They're supposed to be obsessed with "**pretty clothes**", shopping and **weddings** — Sheila gazes adoringly at her ring and asks, "**is it the one you wanted me to have?**"

2) They're **protected** against "**unpleasant and disturbing**" things.

3) Sheila gets Eva sacked because of **pride**, **vanity** and **jealousy** — stereotypical **female** traits in the play.

4) Sheila is accused of being **hysterical** — a state often associated with women at the time.

MEN

1) They're preoccupied with **work and public affairs** — e.g. "**the miners came out on strike**".

2) Gerald feels it's his **duty** to **rescue** Eva/Daisy from the womanising Alderman Meggarty.

3) Gerald is allowed to **sleep around** before his marriage. Sheila isn't. Arthur says that even in his day they "**broke out and had a bit of fun sometimes**". There are **different rules** for men and women.

The young women challenge the stereotypes

Eva/Daisy and Sheila try to rebel and **break out** of the roles that society has given them.

- Eva/Daisy **questioned** the decision of her **boss** and "**had a lot to say**" about wages at the factory.
- Instead of **relying** on a man to **save** her, Eva/Daisy refused to accept Eric's **stolen money**.
- Sheila **interrupts** and **challenges** everyone at different times, apart from the Inspector.

By the end the stereotypes are turned upside down

1) As the play develops Birling, Gerald and Eric get **weaker**, while Sheila gets **stronger**. Priestley does this to **challenge** the audience's view of women at the time.

2) Gerald's **rejected** by Sheila, and Eric is revealed to be **nervous** and **lazy**, with a **drinking problem**. Birling suffers the most — the whole night has slowly undermined his **authority**. He's "*panic-stricken*" as he speaks the **final line** — a very **different** man from the one at the beginning.

© Simon Gough Photography

3) Sheila starts stating **her own opinions**, not those she is 'supposed' to have — "**That's what's important — and not whether a man is a police inspector or not.**" She's learnt to **think for herself**.

EXAM TIP

Mention that the Birlings judge people on their gender...

Impress the examiner by explaining how the Birlings look at class, gender and even clothes to judge people. Stereotypes help them decide who they like and don't like before getting to know them.

Judgement

Priestley makes the end of the play quite a mystery — it's a bit of a cliffhanger. Apart from making the play more exciting, it leaves the audience to figure out what has happened, and more importantly, who to judge.

The style is like an old morality play

An Inspector Calls is like a murder mystery — but it's also like a **morality play**.

1) Morality plays were **religious plays** written in the late Middle Ages. They tried to **teach** people **how to behave** and were **warnings** against the dangers of sin.

2) *An Inspector Calls* follows the **same kind of idea** as these morality plays — it **points** out everyone's **sins**, and tries to get them to **confess**, **repent** and "<u>share</u>" their "<u>guilt</u>".

3) This play is different from the old morality plays, because it doesn't follow **Christian** ideas. The moral judge isn't **God**, it's a police inspector. Priestley makes his morality play **secular** (not religious).

4) The Inspector represents **temporal law** (law courts not based on religion) — but in the end it turns out that it's not a legal issue — it's a **moral one**.

> **Writer's Technique**
>
> **Morality plays** focus on the **seven deadly sins** — pride, greed, lust, envy, gluttony, anger and sloth.

> **TARGET GRADE** 8-9
>
> You could write about the influence of other genres on the play too. For example, the play conforms to many of the conventions of the detective fiction genre — there's a 'crime' to be solved and a 'genius' detective who pieces together the facts. However, *An Inspector Calls* isn't a typical detective story — the action builds to a climax, but there are still mysteries to be solved by the end.

There's something odd about the Inspector

1) Sheila says she had an idea "<u>all along</u>" that "<u>there was something curious about him</u>" and questions the **supernatural** side of the whole thing — she asks **what** he was, not **who** he was.

2) His origin is **unknown**, and he appears **omniscient** (all-knowing) — they didn't tell him anything he didn't already know. It seems **unbelievable** that a real inspector would know so many details.

3) Priestley **deliberately** leaves questions about the Inspector **unanswered**, as it increases the **mystery** and the feelings of tension within the play (see p.20).

© Simon Gough Photography

The important thing is to learn the lesson

1) In the end, it **doesn't matter** who the Inspector is. He teaches the Birlings a lesson — what matters most is how they react to it and which of them learn from it.

- Gerald, Arthur and Sybil decide it was a **hoax**. They're **relieved** that the Inspector was a **fraud** — they think they've been let **off the hook**.

- Sheila and Eric **waver slightly** when they find out there was no **suicide**, but they've **learnt** the important lesson — even if their story didn't have the tragic ending it **might** have done.

2) Sheila and Eric hold true to their **moral instincts** — even when they're given an opportunity to **pretend** "<u>everything's just as it was before</u>". The others, however, act **selfishly** and never take **responsibility** for their actions.

> **KEY QUOTE**
>
> ## "You admit being prejudiced against her case?"
>
> The final thing that doomed Eva/Daisy was Sybil's judgement that she was unworthy of charity. The Inspector reverses that process — suddenly it's Sybil, and the rest of the Birling family, who are being judged. Sneaky.

Learning about Life

This play presents a harsh world. It's not a world for innocent people. You've got to learn fast. Some innocents — like Eva/Daisy's baby — die without ever having a chance.

Some people never learn...

Theme — Young and Old
This is **ironic** — it's mainly the **older generation** who think they **know it all**.

1) Birling **sneers** at Eric's private education and the younger generation who "**know it all**", because he's worked his way up.

2) This **arrogance** is the reason why Birling is so **stubborn**. He doesn't think anyone has anything of use to tell him — especially not his **children** or a lowly **inspector**. He only listens to Gerald because he's from a **higher social class**.

3) Arthur, Sybil and Gerald's arrogance **prevents** them from **changing**. They don't see anything **wrong** in the way they think or act. They believe that **they know best**. Mr Birling's views are made clear in **Act One** and they don't change.

... others try to change

1) The Inspector has much **more** of an effect on Eric and Sheila, who are **ashamed** of their behaviour. They **reject their parents** who have refused to **learn** from the night's events.

2) They understand that the **important thing** about the evening was the **lesson learnt**, not whether the Inspector was **real**.

3) Before they even realise they're involved with the girl's death, they **criticise** their **father's behaviour**.

4) Sheila changes not only her views but also her **personality** — she starts out playful, self-centred and "*pleased with life*", but as the play progresses, her character **dramatically develops** and she becomes more aware, sensitive and mature.

© Simon Gough Photography

Ignorance is bliss

1) One of the reasons that the older generation refuse to change is that they're **happy** living in **ignorance**. The problems of the working class don't **affect them**, so they **don't want to know**.

2) In fact, they don't like to think about anything **troubling**:

  • Prostitution — "**I see no point in mentioning the subject,**" says Birling.
  • Womanising — "**you don't mean Alderman Meggarty?**" says Mrs Birling, even though it's well known.
  • Drinking — "**It isn't true**" says Mrs Birling when Eric's habit is revealed.

3) Even Sheila tries to **forget** her bad behaviour — "**it didn't seem to be anything very terrible at the time.**"

4) They do everything they can to **avoid changing**, even when it's clear that they've done wrong — they refuse to believe it, and **blame everyone else** instead.

5) It **suits them** to think that they're always right — they don't see the point of changing or learning from their night's ordeal. The system **works in their favour**.

"You and I aren't the same people who sat down to dinner"

Although she's no longer angry at Gerald, and respects him for finally telling the truth, Sheila knows the Inspector's visit has changed them both. She accepts her mistakes, and can't just go back to her old life.

Social Responsibility

The play's purpose is to show the importance of social responsibility — the idea that people should act in a way that helps less privileged people rather than hurting them.

The characters' views are challenged

Birling...
... thinks that community responsibility is "**nonsense**". The **interests** of business are more important than **worker's rights**.

Mrs Birling...
... believes that they have **no responsibility** to the working class — her prejudices are so ingrained that they **can't be changed**.

Sheila...
... realises that getting Eva/Daisy sacked out of spite was **irresponsible** — but she didn't **do** anything about it at the time. The Inspector **challenges** her to **improve** her behaviour.

Eric...
... realises **too late** that his selfish actions were **responsible** for ruining Eva/Daisy's chances of improving **her life**.

Social responsibility is the Inspector's main focus

1) His final speech is **clear** and **to the point** — it's a **summary** of his lesson about **responsibility**.

2) The Inspector wasn't just trying to make the family **feel guilty** for Eva Smith, but to **make them aware** of the difficulties faced by all the "<u>millions of Eva Smiths and John Smiths</u>".

> All the events in *An Inspector Calls* are **connected**. Priestley's **moral** seems to be that it doesn't take great people to change the world — we all change it **every day** just by the way we treat others.

> **TARGET GRADE 8-9**
>
> There are different types of responsibility at work in the play. The Inspector wants people to be "responsible for each other". He sees responsibility as a duty towards others. In contrast, Mr and Mrs Birling are only interested in finding out who is "responsible" for the scandal that's going to emerge. To them, responsibility is about individual blame, rather than collective good.

The play reveals a lot about Priestley's socialist ideas

1) Priestley was a supporter of **socialism** — his plays **promote** social responsibility and **criticise** the problems caused by the **class divide**.

2) *An Inspector Calls* tries to make the audience **question** not only their **social responsibility**, but also how **responsible** they are for their own actions.

3) The audience are already wary of Birling's **short-sighted** opinions, so when he criticises socialism, the audience are more likely to **disagree** with him. In this way Priestley uses Birling to **promote** socialist ideas:

- During his speech at the start, Birling says that the whole world will have "<u>peace and prosperity</u>" except "<u>Russia</u>". Russia became a **socialist state** in 1917, and Priestley was **interested** in seeing how successful this was in creating greater **equality** for the Russian people. The first production of *An Inspector Calls* was held in Moscow in 1946.

- Birling attacks George Bernard Shaw and H.G. Wells, who were **well-known socialist writers** during that time — just like Priestley in the 1940s.

EXAM TIP

Show that you understand Priestley's main message...

Priestley is a bit preachy (not surprising given his surname) but that's the point of the play. He wants to spread his ideas about social responsibility as far as he can, so show the examiner that you understand this.

Section Three — Context and Themes

Practice Questions

Priestley lived through two world wars, where people fought to defend Great Britain. With *An Inspector Calls*, he seems to be asking "What sort of society are we trying to defend?" and "Is it worth defending?". But don't worry — these quick questions aren't half as tough as that. They're just supposed to get you thinking.

Quick Questions

1) List two things that were different in 1912 compared to today.

2) What happened in 1914 that would change Britain forever?

For even more practice, try the An Inspector Calls Sudden Fail Quiz — just scan this QR code!

Inspector Quiz

3) List three events that changed the social structure in Britain between 1914 and 1945.

4) Which class is represented in the play by each of the following characters?
   a) Gerald   b) Arthur Birling   c) Eva Smith

Did you expect me to dance?

5) Describe how middle-class women were expected to behave in 1912.

6) Find two quotations in the play that suggest Eric feels left out of family life.

7) List two positions of authority that Mr Birling has held.

8) How do Eric and Sheila rebel against their parents towards the end of the play?

9) What is a morality play?

10) Which other socialist writers does Priestley mention in Arthur Birling's speech about business and industry?

In-depth Questions

1) How does Priestley's presentation of the Birlings make you feel about the middle classes in 1912?

2) Does the Inspector fit into a social class? Explain your answer.

3) Joe Meggarty is an alderman and also a "notorious womanizer". What do you think Priestley is trying to say about 'respectable' society by telling us about this character?

4) At the start of the play, the characters form a clear hierarchy, with Arthur Birling at the top and Eva/Daisy at the bottom. Priestley uses the events of the play to rearrange this hierarchy. How do you think things stand at the end of the play?

5) Do you think Sheila conforms to the gender stereotype for middle-class women in 1912?

6) Why do you think the real identity of the Inspector is never revealed? Does it matter that we don't find out who he really is?

7) What effect do you think the final revelation (that a girl has died after drinking disinfectant and an inspector is on his way) will have on each of the characters?

8) As the Inspector carries out his investigation, the Birling family becomes more and more divided between the old and the young. Find some quotes which show where Gerald fits in.

Practice Questions

Questions about themes can be trickier than ones about plot and characters, so make sure you get plenty of practice by having a go at these questions. Remember to use quotations from the text to back up your answers.

Target Grade 8-9

1) '*An Inspector Calls* is primarily a piece of detective fiction.' How far do you agree?

2) *An Inspector Calls* was written in 1945, but is set in 1912. How might this affect the audience's attitude towards the characters, both in the 1940s and in the present day?

3) "Birling: Sheila, take your mother along to the drawing-room". How far do the female characters allow themselves to be controlled by the male characters throughout the play?

Exam-style Questions

1) What is the significance of the theme of judgement in *An Inspector Calls*?

2) 'Eva Smith shows how society sees innocence as something to take advantage of.'
    How does Priestley present the theme of innocence in the play?

3) How does Priestley show the problems caused by the class system in *An Inspector Calls*?
    Think about:
    • what problems are caused by the class system
    • how Priestley presents the class system.

4) Explore the theme of conflict between the generations in *An Inspector Calls*.

5) Look at Act Two, from Mrs Birling's line "**Women of the town?**" to Birling's line "**Sheila!**"
    With reference to this passage and the play as a whole, how does Priestley use
    the Birlings to explore the theme of ignorance within the middle classes?

6) **Birling [*angrily to Eric*]: You're the one I blame for this.**
    What is the importance of blame and guilt in *An Inspector Calls*?

7) 'Sheila's views on social responsibility have been permanently changed.'
    How does Priestley present the theme of social responsibility in the play?

8) How are the relationships between men and women explored in *An Inspector Calls*?
    Think about:
    • the important relationships between men and women in the play
    • how Priestley presents the relationships.

'An Inspector Calls' on the Stage

An Inspector Calls is a play — don't call it a book or a novel. Priestley wrote it for the stage — to be seen and heard and performed. These pages should help explain how to go about discussing a dramatic text.

One set can be used for the whole play

This diagram is a **plan** of the set used in the **first** production of *An Inspector Calls*, in 1946.

1) All the action takes place in the "*dining-room of a fairly large suburban house*" — so the **whole play** can be staged using one set (though it doesn't have to be).

2) Priestley's design helps make the **atmosphere** of the play seem more **claustrophobic** and **intense**. The room's like a kettle, just about to boil.

A room that makes you feel trapped in a small space is described as 'claustrophobic'.

3) It emphasises the Birlings' **private** and **self-centred** lifestyle and highlights the **unwelcome arrival** of the Inspector who brings bad news from **outside**.

There are warning signs from the very beginning

1) A good production of the play should show the family **falling apart** as their secrets are revealed.

2) At the beginning the audience should see that there are **signs of problems**:

- The actor playing **Sheila** should follow the stage directions "*half serious, half playful*" to make it clear that although she's **joking** with Gerald, she's **not convinced** he's telling her the **truth** about last summer.

- The actor playing **Eric** needs to **balance** his **performance** as a troubled, **regular drinker**, so that he doesn't seem too **sober**, but doesn't seem too **drunk**. This **unsettles** the audience because it's clear that something's **not quite right**.

The way the play looks can say a lot about its message

1) The play takes place in **one room** — suggesting the characters have **closed themselves off** from the world, with their **close-minded** behaviour.

2) The **lighting** is "*pink and intimate*" at the start, as if the Birlings are looking through 'rose-tinted glasses'. But it becomes "*brighter and harder*" when the Inspector arrives — as if a **spotlight** is turned on their cosy world.

Writer's Technique

Priestley's **stage directions** say how the play should look. But **productions** can change the **set**, **lighting** and **costumes** to suit their 'take' on the play.

3) The Birlings and Gerald look **wealthy**. This should be clear from their clothes and furniture. It's part of the **image** they present to society. In **contrast**, Inspector Goole looks **relatively plain**.

4) **Stephen Daldry's** production (first performed 1992) had an **unusual set**. The house was set on **stilts**, high above a street. The **height** showed their **separation** from the rest of the town, but the stilts made the house seem **unsteady** — suggesting that the Birlings' **high status** could easily **collapse**. Because the play wasn't just set in **one room**, the audience is reminded to think about the **world outside**.

Consider how the play would be presented on stage...

Look closely at everything — from lighting instructions to set design, and even the stage directions that say Mrs Birling speaks "*triumphantly*". It's all part of the play, so don't forget to write about it in the exam.

Dramatic Techniques in 'An Inspector Calls'

Think of Priestley as an engineer — he's built the structure of the play with careful precision. He increases the tension and brings the action to an emotional climax using dramatic techniques.

Priestley paces the action to build tension and create conflict

1) At the beginning of Act Two, the audience **expects** the story to move on to Gerald's confession. But instead, Priestley **delays** the action by **shifting** the audience's **attention** to Sybil and Sheila, insisting that they should be allowed to hear what Gerald says. This **builds tension** and **increases** the audience's **curiosity**.

2) Priestley also increases tension by having the Inspector **release information** bit by bit. He shows the photo(s) to **one person** at a time and **positions himself** so the others can't see — the characters, like the audience, are kept **on their toes**.

3) The family all start **seated**, but by the end there are people **standing**, shouting, drinking and crying. As the play goes on, there's a dramatic but slow **change** in how the stage **looks** and **sounds** — this reflects the build-up of "_nervous tension_" among the Birlings.

TARGET GRADE 8-9

Writing about Priestley's use of props, like the photo, can help you to pick up valuable marks in the exam. For example, the telephone is important because it's one of the few links between the Birlings and the outside world. The final phone call represents the intrusion of reality into the new fantasy the Birlings are creating.

Entrances and exits are really important

1) An exit can signal a character **escaping** someone or something — e.g. Sheila "_runs out_" of the room when she realises she's the reason Eva was sacked. She wants to leave the **intense atmosphere** — but she's also running away from **telling her story**.

2) The Inspector uses exits to help draw **information** out of the other characters — e.g. he leaves Sheila and Gerald **alone** to discuss Daisy Renton.

3) The front door **bangs** every time someone **leaves** or **enters** the house. The characters on stage and the audience **hear** this — and wonder **who's** coming and going.

The beginnings and ends of acts are dramatic

Priestley **freezes the action** between Acts to create **tension**.

© Simon Gough Photography

- Act One ends with the Inspector asking "_Well?_". Act Two opens with the **same moment**. The **audience** will wonder about the answer to his question during the break, which **builds the suspense**.

- The end of Act Two is another **cliffhanger**. The front door **slams**, announcing Eric's return, but Priestley makes the audience **wait** until Act Three for **Eric's confession**.

Talk about the ways that Priestley creates drama...

If you just look at the plot in terms of action and events, it seems as if nothing happens — it's just people in a room. But Priestley's dramatic techniques draw out the Birlings' stories like flashbacks in a film.

The Language of 'An Inspector Calls'

The words a character uses can say a lot about their mood or their social class. Priestley's choice of words, the director's decisions about performance and the actor's interpretation of Priestley's tone can all play a part.

The characters' language reveals more about them

The Birlings use words that were popular with middle- and upper-class people in 1912:

* Words such as "chaps" (men) and "jingo" help show the characters' social class. It also suggests that the characters feel comfortable with each other — they're using the language of their social group.

* Some slang words were popular with the younger generation but weren't used by their more old-fashioned parents. Sybil's shocked when Sheila says "squiffy".

* Birling sees the world as a businessman views his company. When Birling realises the Inspector's visit was a "hoax" he uses business language to describe being fooled: "an elaborate sell!" The fact that his language links sales with tricks suggests he might not be an honest businessman either.

Inspector Goole uses language differently

1) The Inspector doesn't mess about. He speaks his mind — e.g. he says Eva/Daisy was burnt "inside out" by disinfectant. This contrasts with Birling's long waffly speech at the beginning of Act One.

2) The Inspector uses plain and direct language, he only says what he needs to — there can't be any confusion.

3) He also uses silence — he has a "disconcerting habit" of staring for a while at a person before he speaks to them.

4) The older Birlings find him offensive because of his manner and language — he is "rude" and "impertinent".

© Donald Cooper/Shutterstock

Sheila's language changes during the play

1) At the start of the play Sheila uses simple and childish language — e.g. she says, "I'm sorry, Daddy," when she's admiring her ring instead of listening to her father.

2) By the end of the play she's confident and assertive. She uses simple, plain and sometimes blunt English, just like the Inspector — e.g. "we drove that girl to commit suicide."

Writer's Technique
Priestley makes Sheila's voice sound full of emotion — her language seems honest and from the heart.

3) She directly disagrees with her parents. She tells them they're wrong to think the Inspector was a "joke" and points out that they "began to learn something" before they decided it was a hoax.

KEY QUOTE **"his manner was quite extraordinary; so — so rude —"**
When the Birlings are beginning to think that the Inspector might have been a fake, his attitude is the first thing that Sybil picks up on. Goole's tone and language make him stand out from the other characters.

50

Language Techniques in 'An Inspector Calls'

Priestley uses little language tricks to give different possible meanings to what his characters are saying. Just one carefully crafted sentence can tell the audience lots of things at once.

Priestley uses dramatic irony to influence the audience

1) It seems as if the Inspector's **omniscient** — he knows everything.

2) Priestley gives similar **power** to the **audience**. He set the play in **1912**, but the play was first performed in **1945**. The audience know that a lot of what Birling dismisses in his speech **actually happened**.

3) When the audience know more than the characters, it's called **dramatic irony**.

4) There's more **irony** in Act One. Birling talks about getting a **knighthood** unless there's a "_scandal_". He jokes "_complacently_" (as if nothing will happen) but the play's title reveals that something **will** happen — an **inspector will call**.

Writer's Technique

Priestley uses dramatic irony to make Birling look **short-sighted** (see pages 6 and 22).

The Birlings use euphemisms to hide what they mean

1) A euphemism is a way of **avoiding** saying something **unpleasant** by using other, often more vague, words.

- Eva/Daisy "_went on the streets_" where she led "_another kind of life_" with the "_women of the town_". These euphemisms hint that she became a **prostitute**.

- To Mrs Birling, Eva/Daisy is a "_girl of that sort_" (she means a lower-class girl), and is in a particular "_condition_" (pregnant).

2) The Inspector doesn't use **euphemisms**. His **language** is more **direct**.

Theme — Learning about Life

Part of the Inspector's message is about **accepting** the **truth**. Using euphemisms does the **opposite** — it **covers** things up.

The Inspector uses imagery

1) Language that creates a **strong picture** is called **imagery**.

2) The Inspector uses **graphic imagery** to shock — the words "_Burnt her inside out_" create an **image** that distresses Sheila and the **audience**.

3) The Inspector's final speech uses **imagery** from the Bible. This makes the Inspector sound like a religious figure:

- "_We are members of one body_" is an idea found in the Bible and the Inspector uses similar phrasing to suggest we have a '**sacred**' duty to care for one another.

- The words "_fire and blood and anguish_" sound like the end of the world described in the Book of Revelation, where "_fire mingled with blood_" rains down — people are punished for their sins.

This cartoon from Punch magazine shows Alastair Sim, who played the Inspector in a 1954 film, as an angel with a flaming umbrella. In the Bible an angel with a flaming sword casts Adam and Eve out of the garden of Eden.

KEY QUOTE **"then they will be taught it in fire and blood and anguish."**
The Inspector's final speech has lots of imagery in it, because Priestley wants the audience to remember it. It's easy to get caught up in the action of the play, but don't forget to look at how language is used, too.

Section Four — The Writer's Techniques

Practice Questions

So, you've thought about the way the play looks and sounds on stage — now try your hand at some of these quick questions. Don't spend too much time answering them — and if you can't remember the answer, go back through this section to remind yourself. Then tackle the in-depth ones. They're a bit trickier.

Quick Questions

1) What is the effect of having one set for the whole play?

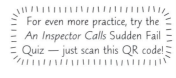 For even more practice, try the *An Inspector Calls* Sudden Fail Quiz — just scan this QR code!

Inspector Quiz

2) What are the two stage directions that show how the lighting should change over the course of the play?

3) Give one example of how Priestley delays the action to build tension.

4) The Birlings all start off seated and well behaved. How does this change over the course of the play?

5) Find two examples of language that reveals the speaker's social class in the play.

6) Why is it important that the front door slams every time someone comes in or goes out?

7) What does the Birlings' use of words like "by jingo" and "squiffy" say about them?

8) What is a euphemism? Give three examples of euphemisms used in *An Inspector Calls*.

9) The Inspector predicts that men will be taught their lesson "in fire and blood and anguish". What religious ideas might this be referring to?

10) Name two differences in the way that the Inspector speaks compared to the Birlings.

In-depth Questions

1) Why do you think Priestley gave stage directions about the lighting effects?

2) How does Priestley use irony for dramatic effect in the play?

3) Look at the stage directions for the Inspector in Act One. Explain the effect his actions have on the other characters.

4) Briefly sketch a set layout for a new production of *An Inspector Calls*. Explain the effect your design is intended to create.

5) Find some examples that show how Sheila's language changes during the play and explain how this changes your opinion of her character.

6) Why is it important that the Inspector uses powerful imagery in his final speech, while the Birlings' language tends to be more down-to-earth?

7) If you were directing a production of *An Inspector Calls*, and had decided to have Eva/Daisy on stage, what sort of costume would you choose for her? Explain your answer.

Practice Questions

Right — bring on the big guns. It's likely that you'll need to show awareness of stagecraft and the writer's techniques in your exam. Even if the exam question doesn't specifically mention it, it's good to show that you're aware of *An Inspector Calls* as a play rather than just a story. Have a think about how the stagecraft fits in with your other ideas about the play — if you do this, you'll find these questions easy as pie.

Target Grade 8-9

1) Do you agree with Stephen Daldry's decision to extend the set design to include the street and other locations mentioned in the play? What do you think is gained and lost by this decision?

2) How does Priestley use props to create tension and change the pace of the action in *An Inspector Calls*? Write about at least two props.

3) The Inspector tells the Birlings that all people "are members of one body". Why is it significant that Priestley uses the image of a "body" to describe humanity? Explain your answer.

Exam-style Questions

1) **Mrs Birling: I must say his manner was quite extraordinary; so — so rude — and assertive —**
   How does Priestley use language in the play to show the differences between characters?

2) Read Act Three from the Inspector's line "*Stop!*" to where he makes his final exit.
   With reference to this passage and the play as a whole, explore how
   the Inspector drives the action in *An Inspector Calls*.

3) How does Priestley make *An Inspector Calls* a dramatic, suspenseful play?
   Think about:
   • what techniques Priestley uses to build suspense
   • how the suspense builds as the play develops.

4) How does Priestley's portrayal of Mr and Mrs Birling contribute to the message of the play?
   Think about:
   • what the message of the play is
   • how Priestley presents Mr and Mrs Birling.

5) 'The characters in *An Inspector Calls* rarely say quite what they mean.'
   To what extent does Priestley portray the Birlings as being a trustworthy source of information?

6) **Inspector: Don't worry, Mrs Birling. I shall do my duty.**
   Explore how Priestley's portrayal of the Inspector makes him a moral figure.

7) 'It's clear from the start that everything is not right with the Birlings.'
   How far do you agree with this statement?

The Assessment Objectives

The assessment objectives are the basis for your exams — you need to meet them to get top marks.

The exam questions will test four main skills

1) You will need to show the examiner that you can meet the following **assessment objectives**:

- **Assessment Objective One (AO1)** — show that you have **read** and **understood** the text, and give a **thoughtful**, **personal** response, **picking out** appropriate **examples** and **quotations** to back up your opinions.
- **Assessment Objective Two (AO2)** — **identify** and **explain** features of the text's **form**, **structure** and **language**. Show how the author uses these to create **meanings** and **effects**, using **subject terminology** where relevant.
- **Assessment Objective Three (AO3)** — relate the text to its **cultural, social and historical background**.
- **Assessment Objective Four (AO4)** — write in a **clear**, **well-structured**, **accurate** way. **5%** of the **total marks** in your English Literature exams are for **spelling**, **punctuation** and **grammar**.

Different exam questions test different assessment objectives — see p.54.

2) A good way to **improve exam technique** is to identify objectives you **struggle with** and try to improve them.

3) The table below shows how to meet the assessment objectives at **different grades**. Look at the **differences** between **each grade band**, and think about what you can do to **achieve the higher grades**.

Grade band	Assessment Objective	An answer at this level...
8-9	AO1	• shows an insightful, critical and engaged personal response to the text • supports arguments with well-integrated, highly relevant and precise examples from the text
	AO2	• closely and perceptively analyses in detail how the writer uses language, form and structure to create meaning and affect the audience, using highly relevant subject terminology
	AO3	• gives a detailed, relevant explanation of the relationship between the text and its context
	AO4	• uses highly varied vocabulary and sentence types and accurate spelling and punctuation
6-7	AO1	• shows a critical and observant personal response to the text • supports arguments with integrated, well-chosen examples from the text
	AO2	• includes a thorough exploration of how the writer uses language, form and structure to create meaning and affect the audience, making use of appropriate subject terminology
	AO3	• explores the relationship between the text and its context
	AO4	• uses a wide range of vocabulary and sentence types and fairly accurate spelling and punctuation
4-5	AO1	• shows a thoughtful and clear personal response to the text • integrates appropriate examples from the text
	AO2	• examines how the writer uses language, form and structure to create meaning and affect the audience, making some use of relevant subject terminology
	AO3	• shows an understanding of contextual factors
	AO4	• uses a moderate range of vocabulary and sentence types, without spelling and punctuation errors which make the meaning unclear

Assessment objectives — objectively useful...

Learning the text back-to-front will help you know *what* to write in your answers, but you also need to know *how* to answer the questions — that's where assessment objectives come in useful. Try to keep them in mind as you're revising.

Preparing for the Exam

Getting to know the text will put you at a massive advantage in the exam. It's not enough just to know the text really well though — you've also got to get familiar with the exam paper if you want to do well.

Make sure you know what your exam looks like

1) There are some **differences** between how each **exam board examines** *An Inspector Calls*. For example, different exam boards test different assessment objectives in each question. You don't want to **waste time** trying to meet an assessment objective that **won't gain you marks**.

2) Check which exam board you're **entered** for and then have a look at the **table below**:

	AQA	Edexcel	Eduqas	OCR
Paper	Paper 2	Paper 1	Paper 2	Paper 1
Total time	2 hours 15 minutes	1 hour 45 minutes	2 hours 30 minutes	2 hours
Time for *An Inspector Calls*	45 minutes	50 minutes	45 minutes	1 hour 15 minutes
Question structure	One question about the whole text	One question about the whole text	One question about an extract <u>and</u> the whole text	One two-part question. Part a) about two extracts, part b) about another moment in the text
Assessment objectives	AO1, AO2, AO3, AO4	AO1, AO3, AO4	AO1, AO2, AO4	AO1, AO2, AO3
Total marks	34	40	40	40

Preparation is important

1) It's **important** to cover **all** the **different sections** of this book in your **revision**. You need to make sure you **understand** the text's **plot**, **characters**, **themes**, **context** and **writer's techniques**.

2) In the **exam**, you'll need to **bring together** your **ideas** about these topics to answer the question **quickly**.

3) Think about the different **characters** and **themes** in the text, and write down some **key points** and **ideas** about each one. Then, find some **evidence** to support each point — this could be something from **any** of the **sections** in this book. You could set out your evidence in a **table** like this:

Theme: Social Class	
Strict class structure	Rigid class structure in England in 1912. Differences between Gerald Croft, the Birlings, and Eva/Daisy.
Difficulties of being lower class	Eva/Daisy struggles to make an honest living. There are "millions and millions and millions of Eva Smiths".
Responsibility of upper and middle classes	The actions of the Birlings and Gerald cause Eva/Daisy's death. Priestley's message of social responsibility.

Preparing to succeed — a cunning plot indeed...

Knowing the plot inside-out will be unbelievably helpful in the exam. It'll help you to stay calm and make sure you write a brilliant answer that positively glitters with little gems of evidence. The exam's just a chance for you to show off...

The Exam Question

This page deals with how to approach an exam question. The stuff below will help you get started on a scorching exam answer, more scorching than, say, a phoenix cooking fiery fajitas in a flaming furnace.

Read the question carefully and underline key words

1) The style of question you'll get depends on which **exam board** you're taking.

2) Read all the **instructions** carefully. Make sure you know **how many** questions you need to answer and **how much time** you should spend answering each one.

3) If the question has **more than one part**, look at the total number of marks for each bit. This should help you to plan your **time** in the exam.

4) **Read** the question at least **twice** so you completely understand it. **Underline** the key words. If you're given an **extract**, underline **important** words or phrases in that too.

Henry didn't read the weather report carefully enough when planning his weekend activities.

Here's an example of an exam-style question:

'**How** questions' ask you to think about the writer's **techniques**. E.g. Priestley's use of **language** and **stage directions**.

Generational conflict is a key **theme** — use a range of examples to support your answer.

You must **refer to** and **quote from** the whole text in your answer.

Q1 <u>How</u> does Priestley explore the theme of <u>conflict</u> <u>between generations</u> in *An Inspector Calls*?

Think about:
- the views of different generations
- how Priestley <u>presents</u> different generations.

Remember to write about **form**, **structure** and **language**.

Some exam boards will give you an extract or a quote from the text to write about. Make sure you read the instructions carefully.

Get to know exam language

Some **words** come up time and again in **exam questions**. Have a look at some **specimen** questions, pick out words that are **often used** in questions and make sure that you **understand** what they mean. You could **write a few down** whilst you're revising. For example:

Question Word	You need to...
Explore / Explain	Show **how** the writer deals with a **theme**, **character** or idea. Make several **different** points to answer the question.
How does	Think about the **techniques** or **literary features** that the author uses to get their point across.
Give examples	Use **direct quotes** and describe **events** from the text in your own words.
Refer to	Read the question so that you know if you need to write about just an **extract**, or an extract and the **rest of the text**.

The advice squad — the best cops in the NYPD...

Whatever question you're asked in the exam, your answer should touch on the main characters, themes, structure and language of the text. All the stuff we've covered in the rest of the book in fact. It's so neat, it's almost like we planned it.

Planning Your Answer

I'll say this once — and then I'll probably repeat it several times — it is absolutely, completely, totally and utterly essential that you make a plan before you start writing. Only a fool jumps right in without a plan...

Plan your answer before you start

1) If you plan, you're less likely to forget something **important**.

2) A good plan will help you **organise** your ideas — and write a good, **well-structured** essay.

3) Write your plan at the **top of your answer booklet** and draw a **neat line** through it when you've finished.

4) **Don't** spend **too long** on your plan. It's only **rough work**, so you don't need to write in full sentences. Here are a few **examples** of different ways you can plan your answer:

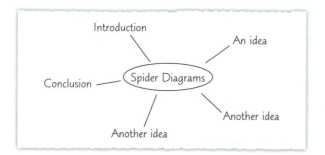

Bullet points...

• Introduction...
• An idea...
• The next idea...
• Another idea...
• Yet another idea...
• Conclusion...

Include bits of evidence in your plan

1) **Writing** your essay will be much **easier** if you include **important quotes** and **examples** in your plan.

2) You could include them in a **table** like this one:

3) **Don't** spend **too long** writing out quotes though. It's just to make sure you **don't forget** anything when you write your answer.

A point...	Quote to back this up...
Another point...	Quote...
A different point...	Example...
A brand new point...	Quote...

Structure your answer

Introduction
↓
Middle Section
— paragraphs
expanding
your
argument.
↓
Conclusion

1) Your **introduction** should give a brief answer to the question you're writing about. Make it clear how you're going to **tackle the topic**.

2) The **middle section** of your essay should explain your answer in detail and give evidence to back it up. Write a **paragraph** for each point you make. Make sure you **comment** on your evidence and **explain how** it helps to **prove** your point.

3) Remember to write a **conclusion** — a paragraph at the end which **sums up** your **main points**. There's **more** about introductions and conclusions on the **next page**.

Dirk finally felt ready to tackle the topic.

To plan or not to plan, that is the question...

The answer is yes, yes, a thousand times yes. Often students dive right in, worried that planning will take up valuable time. But 5 minutes spent organising a well-structured answer is loads better than pages of waffle. Mmm waffles.

Writing Introductions and Conclusions

Now you've made that plan that I was banging on about on the last page, you'll know what your main points are. This is going to make writing your introduction and conclusion as easy as pie.

Get to the point straight away in your introduction

1) First, you need to **work out** what the question is **asking you** to do:

How is the character of Sheila important to the play?

The question is **asking you** to think about the **importance** of **Sheila** in the text.
Plan your essay by thinking about **how** Sheila **links** to the play's **plot** and main **themes**.

2) When you've **planned** your essay, you should **start** it by giving a **clear answer** to the **question** in a sentence or two. Use the **rest** of the **introduction** to **develop** this idea. Try to include the **main paragraph ideas** that you have listed in your plan, but **save** the **evidence** for later.

3) You could also use the **introduction** to give your **opinion**. Whatever you do, make sure your introduction makes it **clear** how your answer **fits the question**.

Your conclusion must answer the question

1) The **most important** thing you have to do at the **end** of your writing is to **summarise** your answer to the question.

2) It's your **last chance** to persuade the examiner, so make your **main point** again.

3) Use your **last sentence** to really **impress** the **examiner** — it will make your essay **stand out**. You could **develop** your own **opinion** of the text or **highlight** which of your **points** you thought was the most **interesting**.

The examiner was struggling to see the answer clearly.

Use the exact question words in your introduction and conclusion

1) Try to use **words** or **phrases** from the **question** in your introduction and conclusion.

How does Priestley use dramatic irony in the play?

2) This will show the examiner that you're **answering the question**.

Priestley uses dramatic irony in 'An Inspector Calls' to show that the character Arthur Birling is not as wise as he pretends to be, and to add humour to the play.

> The first line of the introduction gives a clear answer, which will lead on to the rest of your essay.

3) This will also help you keep the question **fresh in your mind** so your answer doesn't **wander off-topic**.

I've come to the conclusion that I really like pie...

To conclude, the introduction eases the examiner in gently, whilst the conclusion is your last chance to impress. But remember — the examiner doesn't want to see any new points lurking in those closing sentences.

Writing Main Paragraphs

So we've covered the beginning and the end, now it's time for the meaty bit. The roast beef in between the prawn cocktail and the treacle tart. This page is about how to structure your paragraphs. It's quite simple...

P.E.E.D. is how to put your argument together

1) **P.E.E.D.** stands for: **P**oint, **E**xample, **E**xplain, **D**evelop.

2) Begin each paragraph by making a **point**. Then give an **example** from the text (either a quote or a description). Next, **explain** how your example backs up your point.

3) Finally, try to **develop** your point by writing about its effect on the audience, how it links to another part of the text or what the writer's intention is in including it.

Remember to start a new paragraph every time you make a new point.

Use details from the text to back up your points

1) You can use **different** sorts of **examples** to support your points.

2) If you're using a **quote**, try to keep it **short**:

> Sybil is socially "superior" to her husband, which is shown in her strict reinforcement of correct etiquette — she tells him off "reproachfully" for mentioning the servants in front of the more upper-class Gerald, for example.

It's best to use short, embedded quotes as evidence.

Don't just use quotes to describe the plot — it's much better to use them as evidence to support a point you're making.

3) **Quotes** are usually the **clearest** way to illustrate a point, but sometimes you can use a **paraphrased detail instead**. For example, you could briefly describe an **event** in the text:

> The difference in social class between Mr and Mrs Birling sometimes causes conflict. For example, Mrs Birling chastises Mr Birling when he mentions the cook in front of Gerald.

Get to know some literary language

1) Using **literary terms** in your answer will make your essay stand out — as long as you use them correctly.

2) When you're **revising**, think about literary terms that are **relevant** to the text and how you might **include** them in an essay. Take a look at the table below for some examples.

It's not enough to just name a feature — you should explain the effect that it has on the audience.

Literary Term	Definition	Example
Imagery	A description that creates a strong picture.	"Burnt her inside out"
Euphemism	Avoiding saying something unpleasant by using a more vague expression.	"women of the town"
Dramatic irony	When the audience know something that a character doesn't.	"And I say there isn't a chance of war."

This page is so exciting — I nearly...

Now now, let's all be grown ups and avoid the obvious joke. It's a good way of remembering how to structure your paragraphs though. Point, Example, Explain, Develop. Simple. Maybe we could make a rap or something... anyone?

Choosing Quotes

Whether you're looking at an extract or the whole text, quotes can go a long way to support your answer.

Memorise useful quotes for the exam

1) It's really **important** to **learn quotes** that you can use in the exam.
Make yourself a **bank** of quotes and examples that you can use to **support** your answers.

2) Here are some **tips** on how to **choose** the most **useful quotes** to memorise:

   - Choose quotes that are **relevant** to specific **characters** and **themes**
     — exam questions often focus on these topics.

   - Try to pick quotes with a **language** or **structural feature** that you can analyse.

   - Keep your quotes **as short as possible** — **cut out** anything **unnecessary**. This will make
     them **easier to remember** and you'll spend **less time** writing them out in the exam.

3) Here are some **examples** of **useful quotes** that you could include in your quote bank:

This quote is about how the Inspector has judged the Birlings — it can be linked to the theme of judgement.

"He was our police inspector all right."

You could comment on how this quote summarises Eric's perspective about whether or not it matters if the Inspector was a real policeman.

These quotes are short, so it's easy to memorise them.

This is a stage direction for the Inspector. It can be linked to the theme of class and how the Inspector doesn't follow class rules.

"cutting through, massively"

This shows how the Inspector takes control of the room.

It's a good idea to learn some stage directions as well as lines from the play.

In extract questions, find quotes that match the question

1) If you're given an **extract** in the exam, read it **carefully** and **pick out** words or phrases that **link to the question**.

2) Think about what these words and phrases **tell you** about the **topic** you're being
asked to write about. Then use this to form the basis of your exam answer.

3) Focus on the bits of the extract that are **most relevant** to the question — you won't
have time to cover the whole extract, so write about the **most important parts**.

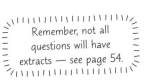

Remember, not all questions will have extracts — see page 54.

4) If you're asked to refer to the **whole text**, remember to
include **examples** that **aren't** from the extract too.

This page is really useful — and you can quote me on that...

Quotes are completely essential to show the examiner that you know the text and can support your arguments.
Don't try to write out half the play though — a short and snappy quote will often serve you better than a long one.

In the Exam

Keeping cool in the exam can be tricky. But if you take in all the stuff on this page, you'll soon have it down to a fine art. Then you can stroll out of that exam hall with the swagger of an essay-writing master.

Don't panic if you make a mistake

1) Okay, so say you've timed the exam beautifully. Instead of putting your feet up on the desk for the last 5 minutes, it's a good idea to **read through** your **answers** and **correct any mistakes**...

2) If you want to get rid of a mistake, **cross it out**. **Don't scribble** it out as this can look messy. Make any corrections **neatly** and **clearly** instead of writing on top of the words you've already written.

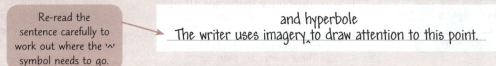

> techniques
> The author uses various literary ~~teknikues~~ to explore this theme.

This is the clearest way to correct a mistake. Don't be tempted to try writing on top of the original word.

3) If you've **left out** a **word** or a **phrase** and you've got space to add it in **above** the line it's missing from, write the missing bit above the line with a '∧' to show exactly where it should go.

Re-read the sentence carefully to work out where the '∧' symbol needs to go.

> and hyperbole
> The writer uses imagery ∧ to draw attention to this point.

4) If you've left out whole **sentences** or **paragraphs**, write them in a **separate section** at the **end** of the essay. Put a **star** (*) next to both the **extra writing** and the **place** you want it to go.

Always keep an eye on the time

1) It's surprisingly **easy** to **run out of time** in exams. You've got to leave **enough time** to answer **all** the questions you're asked to do. You've also got to leave enough time to **finish** each essay properly — with a **clear ending**.

2) Here are some **tips** on how to **avoid** running out of time:

- Work out **how much time** you have for each part of your answer **before** you **start**.
- Take off a few minutes at the beginning of the exam to **plan** your answer, and leave a **few minutes** at the end to write your **conclusion**.
- Keep **checking** the **clock** so you don't lose track of time.
- Be **strict** with yourself — if you spend **too long** on one part of your answer, you may run out of time. **Stick** to your **planned timings** as much as possible.
- If you're **running out of time**, keep **calm**, **finish** the **point** you're on and move on to your **conclusion**.

Stephanie never had a problem with keeping cool.

Treat an exam like a spa day — just relax...

Some people actually do lose the plot when they get into the exam. The trick is to keep calm and well... carry on. If you make sure you get your exam technique sorted, you'll be as relaxed as a sloth in a room full of easy chairs.

Sample Exam Question

And now the bit you've all been waiting for — a sample exam question and a lovely little plan.
Go make yourself a cup of tea, settle down and enjoy.

Here's a sample exam question

Read this feisty exam question. That's the best way to start...

Read the question carefully. Underline the **important bits**.

What **techniques** does Priestley use to **develop** the Inspector's character?

Your ideas should **link** back to the Inspector's **importance** in the play.

Remember to **back up** your points with **evidence** from the text and **analyse** why it's **important**.

Q1 How does Priestley present the Inspector as an important character in the play?
Think about:
- how Priestley presents the Inspector
- the Inspector's function in the play.

Who or **what** is he? What **role** does he play? What's his **purpose**?

Stick to the question in your answer. **General comments** won't impress the examiner.

Here's how you could plan your answer...

Make sure you don't spend too long planning — you need to leave plenty of time to write your answer.

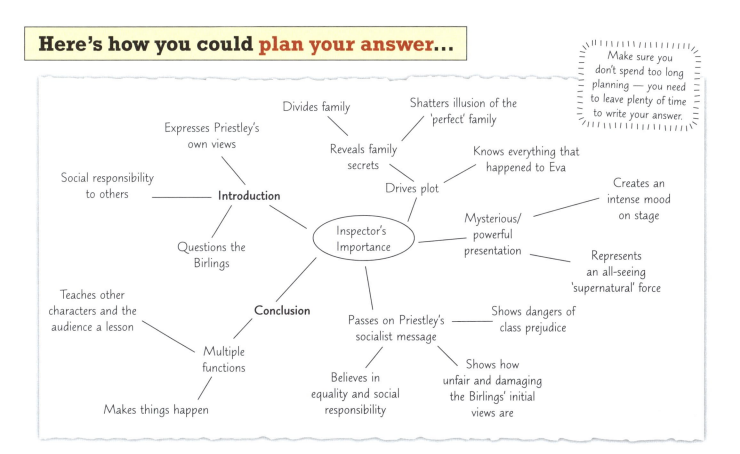

What do examiners eat — eggs-ham-wiches of course...

The most important thing to remember is DON'T PANIC. Take a deep breath, read the questions, pick a good 'un, write a plan... take another deep breath and start writing. Leave 5 minutes at the end to check your answer too.

Worked Answer

These pages will show you how to turn an okay answer into a really good one that will impress the examiner.

Use your introduction to get off to a good start

These pages are all about how to word your sentences to impress the examiner, so we haven't included everything from the plan on page 61.

You might start with something like...

> Priestley's play is intended to make everyone aware of their social responsibility.
> The Inspector is an important character because he is the one to deliver this message.

1) This intro is **okay**. It mentions the **message** of social responsibility and the Inspector's importance.

2) It's also a good idea to use the **key words** in the question (like '**important**') to give your essay **focus** and show the examiner you're on **track** and that you're thinking about the question from the start.

3) But there's still room for **improvement**...

This intro explains the author's message and the point of the play.

> The Inspector is an important character because he is responsible for conveying the key message of *An Inspector Calls* that we should not judge others based on their social class and background. He is also important because his presentation as a mysterious and powerful figure allows him to control the action from the moment he arrives, and he drives the plot by using Eva/Daisy's story to expose the Birlings' guilt.

Introducing your main arguments tells the examiner what the essay's about and shows that you've thought about your essay structure.

Make your first paragraph about the most important point

> The Inspector is important because he presents Priestley's message in a variety of ways. He first highlights the problems of a class-based society. Mrs Birling in particular shows no compassion towards Eva Smith because Eva is working class. Her line "Girls of that class" suggests that she can't even bear to speak the words 'working class'.

1) This paragraph gives an **example** of the problems with class-based societies and mentions the Inspector's role.

2) But... it doesn't **develop** the examples **fully** and it doesn't focus enough on the Inspector's importance.

3) To improve the paragraph, it should have a clearer **structure**, more **detail** and an analysis of the Inspector's role in highlighting the problems with the class-based society.

This is a good start — it tells the examiner what you're going to talk about.

This is good because it includes a detailed example and it analyses and develops the point further.

Make sure you keep referring back to the question by focusing on the Inspector's importance.

> One of the Inspector's most important functions is to put across Priestley's message that it is wrong to judge people based on their social class. In the play, the Birling family represent an outdated, class-obsessed society. Mrs Birling, for example, "didn't believe a word" of Eva's story because she wrongly assumes that having morals is "simply absurd" for working-class women. In contrast, the Inspector's opinions are not clouded by class prejudices. He does not value the same things as the Birlings, for example, he has "never wanted to play" golf. His rejection of class prejudice makes him an important character because it provides a contrast to the Birlings' obsession with class. This highlights how outdated and wrong the Birlings' views are.

Worked Answer

You need to make a variety of points

After you've talked about highlighting social problems you might start your next point like this:

> The Inspector's importance is shown through the way he drives the plot forward by forcing the Birlings to explain their involvement in Eva's death.

1) It introduces **another reason** why the Inspector is an important character.
2) You can make this paragraph better by giving more **detailed examples** and backing up points with **quotes**.

Opening your paragraph with a clear point shows how this paragraph will directly answer the question.

> The Inspector has an important function in driving the plot forward, revealing how all the characters contributed to Eva's death. He appears to know everything because of a "rough sort of diary" that Eva kept. But more importantly, he is in complete control of how information is revealed to the audience. Each character "must wait his turn"; when the Birlings get distracted by their own problems he interrupts "with authority" and forces the dialogue back to the developing story of Eva.

Make sure you use a range of quotes, but don't quote huge chunks. Keep them snappy and relevant.

3) You could develop this further by describing how the Inspector creates conflict between the other characters:

Analysing the language of the play helps support your points.

> As well as revealing facts about Eva's life, the Inspector drives the plot by causing conflict between the other characters. For example, the Inspector causes conflict between Gerald and Sheila by forcing Gerald to confess to his affair. The Inspector's questions, such as "When and where did you first meet her?", are direct and authoritative, leaving Gerald with little choice but to be honest about his relations with Daisy. This is an important moment in the play because it leads Sheila to break off their engagement.

Finish your essay in style

You could say:

> In conclusion, the Inspector is a very important character because he is responsible for delivering Priestley's main message. Priestley portrays him as a powerful character who has an important message to share with the audience.

1) This conclusion's okay but it doesn't summarise **how** Priestley presents the Inspector as important.
2) So to make it really **impressive** you could say something like...

> In conclusion, the Inspector is a very important character because he fulfils many important functions, and his presentation is shaped for these purposes. He drives the plot, forcing out the confessions which move the play to its conclusion, namely that "We are responsible for each other." He stands outside the Birlings' world and can make judgements on the characters along with the audience. He is not just another character; Priestley presents him as omniscient and god-like to aid his function as a judge and a teacher as well as the author's mouthpiece.

Make your last sentence really stand out — it's your last opportunity to impress the examiner.

Why do alligators write good essays? Their quotes are so snappy...

It seems like there's a lot to remember, but it's really quite simple. Just write a good intro and conclusion, make a range of points (one per paragraph) and put your most important point in paragraph one. Easy.

64

Exam Tips

We've scoured examiners' reports and mark schemes, and come up with these tips for doing well. Here's a breakdown of what the markers like to see (cake) and what they don't like to see (Brussels sprouts).

Here are our top 10 things to do in the exam...

1) **Do** make sure you **know the text** really well before you go into the exam.

2) **Do** come up with your own **interpretation** of the text that can be **supported** with evidence.

3) **Do read and reread** any extract really carefully, and check that you're **referring** to it correctly in your answer.

4) **Do plan** your answer. It helps you **organise** your thoughts and give a clear response.

5) **Do** write about **how** an **extract relates** to the text as a whole (**if** you're asked to discuss **both**) — think about **where** in the text it comes, and what happens before and after.

6) **Do** remember to comment on **structure** and **form** as well as language.

7) **Do eat** a really good **breakfast** before the exam (and no engagement parties the night before).

8) **Do** write about **why** the author **chose** to use the **words** they do — think about the **effects** they may have been trying to create.

9) **Do** remember to write about **context** in your answer **if** it's being tested in the question. Make sure the context is **relevant** and **clearly linked** to the text.

10) **Do** use **short quotes** from the text to **save time** and make your answer **clear**.

... and here are our top 10 things not to do

1) **Don't** just **rewrite** an **essay** that you've **written before** the exam — it might not be answering the **question** properly and the points you make might not be **relevant**.

2) **Don't** answer the question that you **wish** had been asked — make sure you **answer the question** that **has** been asked.

3) **Don't just name** the **techniques** being used — you need to **explain** the **effects** they have too.

4) **Don't** jump straight into answering the question **without planning**.

5) **Don't contradict yourself** or change your mind halfway through — this can make your points seem weak. It's fine to **discuss two sides** of an argument, but you need to come to a **clear conclusion** at the end.

6) **Don't** write your whole answer about a specific passage in the text — **unless** the question asks you to.

7) **Don't** write about quotes in a way that **misinterprets** what they mean in the text, and don't **shoehorn** them in when they don't fit your argument. This will make it seem like you don't know the text.

8) **Don't** take a **phone** into your exam — you never know when an Inspector **might call**.

9) **Don't cram** loads of **points** into each paragraph — stick to a structure like P.E.E.D. instead (see p.58).

10) **Don't** include **unnecessary context** if it doesn't link to the question or your argument.

Complete the Plan

Now you know all about what makes a good exam answer, it's time to put your knowledge to the test by making a practice essay plan. Remember that planning your answer carefully is crucial if you want to write a top essay, so take your time with this activity. You'll find answers for this whole section in your Online Edition — to access it, just go to **cgpbooks.co.uk/extras** and enter the code at the front of this book.

Complete the Plan

- Below is an **exam question** and **part of a plan**.
  Draw your **own version** on a separate **piece of paper**.

- Think of **four more points** that could go in the 'Point' column to answer the exam question.

- Find **examples** from the text to back up each of your points for the 'Evidence' column. Make sure you use a **range** of examples from across the text.

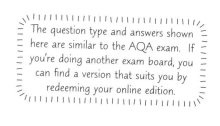

The question type and answers shown here are similar to the AQA exam. If you're doing another exam board, you can find a version that suits you by redeeming your online edition.

- You **don't** need to write the answer itself — just come up with a plan.

- The **first row** has been done for you.

1) How does Priestley use the Birling family to explore the theme of social responsibility?

   Think about:

   - the importance of social responsibility in the play

   - how Priestley portrays members of the Birling family.

Point	Evidence
The younger Birlings disagree with their parents about the importance of social responsibility.	Eric thinks his father acted irresponsibly by sacking Eva Smith. He asks, "Why shouldn't they try for higher wages?"

Remember — you would need to explain and develop your points if you wrote out your answer in full.

Improve the Answer

Now it's time to have a go at choosing examples. Look back at page 59 for advice on selecting quotes.

Add Examples

You can refer to your copy of the play to help you with this question.

- Below are some parts of **sample answers** for another exam-style question.

- Find a **quote** or **example** from the text that could fill each gap below (marked **A-H**).

> 1) How does Priestley use the Inspector as a way of judging the other characters?
>
> Think about:
> - who the Inspector judges in the play
> - how the Inspector's judgement is shown.

1) The Inspector's manner of speaking and interrogation tactics force the Birlings to reveal their faults, enabling the audience to judge them. For example, the Inspector uses very forceful language with Mrs Birling when he asks her about Eva/Daisy. The stage directions describe him as speaking **(A)**, and he repeats questions like **(B)**. This repetition of questions creates an interrogative tone that forces the Birlings to respond, meaning that they reveal their actions to the Inspector. Priestley uses the Inspector to create a picture of each character's motivations and prejudices so they can be judged critically.

2) The contrasting styles of language used by the Inspector and the Birlings lead the audience to judge the characters. The Inspector is extremely blunt and straightforward in his speech. For example, **(C)**. The Birlings, on the other hand, use euphemisms when talking about something they find unpleasant or distasteful. Mrs Birling does this when she refers to Eva/Daisy as **(D)**. Priestley encourages the audience to judge the Birlings unfavourably by comparing their euphemistic and deceitful way of speaking to the honest and plain-speaking style of the Inspector.

3) As well as judging the Birlings directly, the Inspector manipulates the Birlings into judging each other. In Act Two, he uses a series of questions like **(E)** to provoke Sybil into unknowingly blaming Eva/Daisy's death on Eric. Here, the Inspector tricks Sybil into judging Eric for him. At times, he leaves the stage entirely in order to allow the other characters to judge each other, such as **(F)**. The Inspector's absence in moments like this gives the other characters a chance to criticise each other, but it also allows the audience to judge them for the way they behave behind the Inspector's back.

4) Priestley's portrayal of the Inspector as a policeman further encourages the audience to view him as a judge-like character. The Inspector is introduced as a policeman, rather than by name: at the beginning of Act One, Edna says **(G)**. This means the audience immediately sees the Inspector as a character who is there to pass judgement on the Birlings, so the audience is more likely to view the Birlings in a critical way. This is reinforced by the Inspector's language. For example, in Act One, when Mr Birling accuses him of asking unnecessary questions, the Inspector tells him **(H)**. This shows how the Inspector uses his position as a policeman to justify his intense questioning, giving him more power to pass judgement on others.

Improve the Answer

It's time for even more activities on improving answers — this time on developing points and adding context.

Develop the Points

> To develop your point you could write about its effect on the audience, how it links to another part of the text or what the writer's intention is in including it.

- Below are some more parts of **sample answers** for the question on page 66.

- Write an extra sentence that could go in each gap (marked **A-C**) to develop the points.

1) The Inspector comes into the Birling household as an outsider. He is unimpressed by Mr Birling's connections and responds bluntly to Mr Birling's warnings by saying "I don't play golf." This hints that he won't be intimidated or impressed into giving the Birlings special treatment because he does not want to be a part of their world. This means that he is able to take an objective view of the family's actions and then judge them accordingly. **(A)**

2) The Inspector's purpose is not to learn information from the Birlings, but to judge them for their actions so that he can teach them to be better people. Sheila realises that the Inspector knows more than he reveals when she tells Gerald, "I hate to think how much he knows that we don't know yet". Sheila's words imply that the Inspector already knows all the important facts about Eva/Daisy's death, so his aim is not to find out how she died, but to judge the Birlings' reactions to news of her death. **(B)**

3) Priestley's staging of the play adds to the impression that the Inspector has come to judge the other characters. For example, the lighting becomes *"brighter and harder"* when the Inspector arrives. This change in lighting can be seen as a symbol of how the Inspector has come to 'shine a light' on the Birlings' private lives. **(C)**

Add Context

> You might not need to include context (AO3) in your exam on 'An Inspector Calls' — check the table on p.54.

- Below are some more parts of **sample answers** for the question on page 66.

- Write an extra sentence for each gap (marked **A-B**) that links the answer to the context of the play.

1) Priestley presents the Inspector as having an apparently 'supernatural' ability to see the future. This allows him to judge the Birlings because he knows about the "fire and blood and anguish" that mankind is about to suffer in future wars. **(A)** The audience's awareness of the dark future awaiting the Birlings makes the Inspector's words seem damning — he knows what the 'crimes' of people like the Birlings will lead to and has already judged them for it.

2) Unlike the Birlings and Gerald, the Inspector does not appear to come from the upper classes. **(B)** The fact that the Inspector does not fit into this class system is important because it means that he does not share the Birlings' prejudices and assumptions about class. This is shown when he describes Eva/Daisy simply as a "lively sort of girl", without reference to her class. The Inspector's position outside the class system therefore allows him to judge the Birlings by highlighting their prejudices.

Mark the Answer

Here's another sample question, and this time there's a full answer to sink your teeth into (delicious).

Mark the answer

- Below is an exam question and a sample answer.

- The sample answer has been annotated, showing where it has done well or not so well for each assessment objective. Add some more annotations to show what's good and what could be improved.

- Decide whether you think the answer belongs in the grade band **4-5**, **6-7** or **8-9** (see page 53).

- Give at least **three reasons** why you've decided on that grade band.

---

1) How does Priestley present Gerald as a complex character in *An Inspector Calls*?

   Think about:

   - what Gerald says and does

   - how Priestley presents Gerald to the audience.

Gerald is one of the most complex characters in the play. He is both an insider and an outsider in the Birling family, he doesn't fit in to either the older or younger generation and he has a complex attitude to women. It's also unclear how much Gerald is changed by the events of the play.

It is clear from the start of the play that Gerald has a complicated relationship with the Birlings. Mr Birling likes Gerald: he says that he wants to treat him "like one of the family". However, Mr Birling's enthusiasm isn't enough to overcome Sheila's doubts about Gerald's absences in the summer. The stage directions describe Sheila as "half serious, half playful" when she expresses these doubts. In this stage direction, Sheila tries to be "playful", but she is "serious" at the same time. This shows that she has mixed emotions about Gerald and is suspicious about his behaviour. Gerald is therefore a complex character because he isn't an insider in the Birling family, but he isn't an outsider either.

Gerald's complexity as a character is also shown by the fact that he is a member of the younger generation but acts as though he is part of the older generation. At the end of the play, Gerald attempts to prove that the Inspector was not a police officer. The stage direction "decisively" and his line "We can settle this at once" demonstrate that he is a character who, like Mr and Mrs Birling, is more interested in undermineing the Inspector's authority than learning from his own mistakes. In contrast, Eric and Sheila, who repressent the views of the younger generation, feel that they should all learn from their mistakes. Therefore, Gerald plays a complex role in the play because Priestley uses him to show that not all young people are progressive and willing to learn from their mistakes.

> **AO4**: This makes use of a good range of vocabulary but could do more to avoid spelling errors.

The answer continues on the next page...

Mark the Answer

The way that Gerald talks about and acts towards women also makes him complex. Gerald describes the women at the Palace Bar as "hard-eyed" and "dough-faced". His uncomplimentary language is in direct contrast to the way he describes Daisy's "soft brown hair and big dark eyes". This suggests that Gerald judges women according to their looks and not their character. However, Priestley suggests that Gerald's attitude towards women is not entirely shallow. For example, Gerald explains that he originally wanted to help Daisy out of pity for her, rather than because he was looking for an affair. This suggests that his care for Daisy goes beyond finding her physically attractive, which makes him seem like a less shallow and more complex character. Gerald's initial attitude was fairly common at the time: upper-class people in 1912 sometimes looked down on lower-class women, especially prostitutes.

> **AO3**: This shows some understanding of the context that the play was written in, but it could link it to the argument more clearly.

Gerald's emotional reaction to news of Eva/Daisy's death makes him more complex as a character. Gerald tells the Inspector that he is "rather more — upset — by this business than I probably appear to be" and then leaves the stage. His dialogue is broken up by dashes, which suggests that he is struggling to deal with his emotions. It was unusual for upper-class men in 1912 to show their emotions, so Gerald admitting to feeling "upset" is surprising and makes him seem more complex than the stereotype of an upper-class man at the time. By having Gerald leave the stage, Priestley structures the play in a way that draws attention to Gerald's emotions. Therefore, by highlighting Gerald's emotions and showing that he does not always behave like a typical upper-class man, Priestley suggests that Gerald is a complex character.

> **AO2**: This provides some analysis of the play's structure, but could go into more detail.

In conclusion, Priestley uses a variety of techniques to present Gerald as a complex character who doesn't quite fit with many of the stereotypes of 1912. He is both an insider and an outsider in the Birling family, he doesn't fully belong to either the older or younger generation, he has a complex attitude towards women and he is more open about his emotions than many upper-class men were in 1912.

> **AO1**: The conclusion mentions all the points discussed in the essay, but it could do more to bring the argument together.

Index

The Characters from 'An Inspector Calls'

Phew! You should be an expert on *An Inspector Calls* by now. But if you want a bit of light relief and a quick recap of the play's plot, sit yourself down and read through *An Inspector Calls — The Cartoon*...

Arthur Birling

The Inspector

Sybil Birling

Gerald Croft

Eva Smith / Daisy Renton

Eric Birling

Edna

Sheila Birling

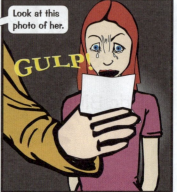